MW01126155

Here's What the World Is Saying About the Kid from Brooklyn

"If Archie Bunker had TiVo, he'd be The Kid from Brooklyn."
—VH1

"The Kid from Brooklyn is a true American original— Lou Costello by way of Ralph Kramden with a little Rodney Dangerfield and Andrew Dice Clay tossed into the mix. He's refreshingly politically incorrect in a world of wimps and not afraid to say what pisses him off no matter who it offends. I love this guy. His rant on Starbucks will have people laughing for the next century."
—Julius Alvin, author of *Mr. K's Book of Really Nasty Jokes*

"This guy is filthy, offensive, and downright disgusting. He reminds me of my husband."
—JoAnn T., Teterboro, New Jersey

"I hope the Kid from Brooklyn really does run for president in 2008. This guy's got balls like coconuts."
—Tony Z, Pittsburgh

"The Kid from Brooklyn doesn't pull his punches and tells it like it is. I wish we had a million more like him, even if it meant a lot less pizza for the rest of us."
—Donnie B., Detroit

"Why doesn't this guy have his own fucking sitcom?"
—Beverly G., Fort Lauderdale, Florida

Go F*** YOURSELF

THE KID FROM BROOKLYN's RANTS AND OTHER STUFF

**MIKE
"THE KID FROM BROOKLYN"
CARACCIOLO**
with MICHAEL BENSON

CITADEL PRESS
Kensington Publishing Corp.
www.kensingtonbooks.com

CITADEL PRESS BOOKS are published by

Kensington Publishing Corp.
850 Third Avenue
New York, NY 10022

Copyright © 2008 Mike Caracciolo

All rights reserved. No part of this book may be reproduced in any form or by any means without the prior written consent of the publisher, excepting brief quotes used in reviews.

All Kensington titles, imprints, and distributed lines are available at special quantity discounts for bulk purchases for sales promotions, premiums, fund-raising, educational, or institutional use. Special book excerpts or customized printings can also be created to fit specific needs. For details, write or phone the office of the Kensington special sales manager: Kensington Publishing Corp., 850 Third Avenue, New York, NY 10022, attn: Special Sales Department; phone 1-800-221-2647.

CITADEL PRESS and the Citadel logo are Reg. U.S. Pat. & TM Off.

First printing: January 2008

10 9 8 7 6 5 4 3 2 1

Printed in the United States of America

CIP data is available.

ISBN 13: 978-0-8065-2865-6
ISBN 10: 0-8065-2865-6

This book is lovingly dedicated to my wife, Mona, who if she had the chance would tell youse all to go fuck yourselves.

DISCLAIMER

All the stories in this book are based on real shit that actually happened. I did change most of the names to keep these dick-weeds from suing my ass. A lot of them are dead now but I happen to know they got some relatives who are still around and are greedy *stoonads* who can smell a buck like a horse can smell water.

Also, I use the f word a lot in the book but it's not for the purposes of shocking anyone—it's just how the Kid from Brooklyn fuckin' expresses himself. If you're offended, tough titty. Read my book or don't read my book. What the fuck do I care?

—Mike Caracciolo
"The Kid from Brooklyn"

Contents

Introduction: Go Fuck Yourself

You know, ladies and gentlemen, people today are afraid. They are afraid to express themselves, afraid to tell their fellow man how they really feel. Our society is close lipped. Mum is the word. It is a time of political correctness, when it is better to hold a pressure cooker's worth of aggravation inside than to risk hurting someone's feelings.

Fuck that.

Me, I'm going to tell you straight out how I feel. I don't give a fuck. And I will be your voice, too. The Voice of the People.

The other day I got a guy on the phone, you know a big-business monkey, and he calls me up and he's giving me a fuckin' hard time. He's bustin' my fuckin' balls. This fuckin' guy's middle name is aggra-fuckin'-vation. I got so fuckin' aggravated with the guy that I said, "Hey! Go fuck yourself! Do you hear me? Go fuck yourself!"

That's what you've got to do today. If you are displeased and you don't like what somebody did, tell 'em: *Go fuck yourself!* That's what everybody should say when they are displeased.

That's what I tell everybody: "Hey! Go fuck yourself! Go fuck yourself sideways, you greedy rat bastard."

Here's another story, from back when I was driving for a car service in Canarsie, where I grew up. I was driving one day and a fuckin' cop—a fuckin' cop!—cut me off. I almost wrecked my fucking car. I had to slam on the fuckin' breaks and fuckin' swerve my car, to not hit the fuckin' cop car. It all happened so fast. I didn't know right away that he was a fucking cop.

I said, "Go fuck yourself!" The guy stopped his car. Got out. I got out. I said, "Go fuck yourself!" You know what the cop did? He went back to the precinct and came to my house with six cop cars.

I got escorted away in handcuffs. The Big Man has got big fuckin' wrists so there was no way the fuckin' cop was going to put those cuffs on loose. They bit right into the skin and pretty soon I couldn't even wiggle my fuckin' fingers.

I went to fuckin' court and the judge was reading off the charge. And the judge said, "Did you tell this officer to go fuck himself?"

I said, "That's right, Judge. I told him to go fuck himself!"

Wound up my lawyer beat the fucking case. Turned out the cop who filed the charge filled out the form wrong. I had to pay a forty-dollar court charge. I felt like telling the judge to go fuck himself.

Because that's what you got to do—when you are displeased with somebody or getting fuckin' aggravated because somebody's fuckin' you up the old wazoo, you just tell 'em to go fuck themselves!

Me, I'm going to tell you straight out how I feel. I don't give a fuck. And I will be your voice, too. The Voice of the People.

Acknowledgments

The Kid from Brooklyn wants to thank some people without whose help the creation of this book would have been impossible. First of all Citadel Press Senior Editor Gary Goldstein, who had the fuckin' vision to realize the Kid was Pulitzer material; Jake Elwell, of Harold Ober Associates, literary agent extraordinaire, and to all the people who put the Kid on the map by visiting www.thekidfrombrooklyn.com and watching my videos. Without you I'd have a fuckin' soapbox but no fuckin' audience. God bless!

" Never try to teach a pig how to dance. It's a waste of your time and annoys the hell out of the pig. "
—Old Sicilian proverb

1. Hand-job Annie and the Flying Baby Batter

Her name was Ann Marie Hanratty, but we all called her Hand-job Annie. You don't have to be a fuckin' Alvin Einstein to figure how she got that nickname.

Annie was a couple of years older than me and my pals, maybe nineteen or twenty. Word around Ninety-second Street was, Hand-job Annie would whack you off for two dollars, anytime, anywhere. Shit, I seen her myself, doing the job on Louie Lombardi in the alley behind Scrappy Bernstein's candy store right there on Avenue K.

Two dollars was a lot of scratch back then, but, as Louie Lombardi told us later, "That Annie can work a dick smoother than one of Scrappy's milk shakes."

I should mention here that Louie was a cheap fuckin' cocksucker. He was so fuckin' cheap he'd shit in a shoe box to save the nickel for a pay toilet. What was even worse, Louie would borrow money and never pay you back. Once he asked me to loan him a dollar. He still owed me six bits for the turtle he sold me that croaked an hour after I got it home, so I told him to go screw. So the little bastard had the fuckin' balls to say I was tight with a buck. Louie, if you're out there someplace reading this, you stingy fuck, yeah, I was tight. So was your sister.

So Louie Lombardi's springing for two bucks for a hand job was better advertising for Annie than a fuckin' neon sign. Pretty soon, every guy in Canarsie with a stiff dick and two bucks was keeping her busy. (She worked as a nurse for old Doctor Bindelbender and always had plenty of rubber gloves and Vaseline for when she was moonlighting.) Don't get me wrong—Annie wasn't no whore. She gave hand jobs but nothing else, no cocksucking or what went after. She was a nice Catholic girl who went to mass every Sunday. Shit, Frankie Coletti once told me how Hand-job Annie belted him in the mouth when he tried to pinch her left tit while she was jerking him off.

The best Hand-job Annie story, though, was the time Sammy Zuckerbrot took her up to do him in the balcony of the Brooklyn Paramount during a matinee of a Dean Martin picture called *Who's Got the Action*, which, come to think about it, sorta makes sense. Sammy saved the two dollars out of his pay from pumping gas at Kronski's Shell station on Tilden Avenue.

Now I got to tell you that Sammy Zuckerbrot was hung bigger than Hopalong Cassidy's fuckin' horse. Jews got a reputation for having tiny dicks but that's a lot of bullshit. Sammy weighed 130 pounds soaking wet, and half of it was cock. It looked like one of those big Hebrew National salamis that used to hang in the window of Pinskey's Kosher Deli. Eddie Fallon one time put a tape measure to it in the locker room. Soft, that monster was eight inches.

"How big does it get when it's hard?" Eddie asked him.

"I don't know," Sammy said. "I always pass out first."

So we called him Sammy the Shmeckle (*shmeckle* being Yiddish for "Jew with a gigantic cock"). Sammy was the biggest and Annie was the best, so I guess it was inevitable that they'd get together. What happened to them became the stuff of Canarsie legend.

It helps to know that the Brooklyn Paramount was a fuckin' palace in its day, with, like, eight hundred seats and

The Brooklyn Paramount theater, a few years before Hand-job Annie did Sammy the Schmeckle in the balcony and all hell broke loose. (Photo courtesy Brian Merlis, www.brooklynpix.com)

a screen two stories high. Used to have vaudeville and big stage shows back when dinosaurs roamed Flatbush Avenue. It's where I saw *Ben-Hur* and *Spartacus* and *Lawrence of Astoria*.

It was a four o'clock show on a Tuesday, so the joint wasn't too crowded. Annie and the Shmeckle had the whole front row of the balcony to themselves.

Annie always made you pay her in advance. How do I know this? None of your fuckin' business, that's how I know. So before the Shmeckle could even get into his fuckin' M&M's, Annie was already getting impatient and started yanking down his zipper.

"This ain't no date, sport," Annie said. "I got another appointment in an hour, so get it out and get it up."

Now this was the first time the Shmeckle ever did anything with his pecker that didn't involve his left hand (the Shmeckle was a southpaw) so he was nervous as a virgin on a Greek freighter. His hands were shaking like he had the fuckin' palsy. Pressed for time, Annie slipped into one of her rubber gloves and reached into the Shmeckle's Fruit of the Looms. When Annie yanked his massive sausage out, she cried, "Jesus, Mary, and Joseph—it's bigger than Rhode Island."

She demanded another dollar. The Shmeckle hadn't planned for any unexpected developments like this. He only had some pocket change—two dimes, two pennies, and his lucky quarter. (Though it wasn't too fuckin' lucky for him that day, as you're gonna see.)

Hand-job Annie settled for the forty-seven cents and the rest of his M&M's.

The Shmeckle was worried he wouldn't be able to get

his rope to rise—this wasn't exactly how he imagined his first fuckin' sex encounter would be—but Annie was a pro and she had his *shvantz* standing at full attention in a heartbeat. Plus, Sammy confided later, "I shut my eyes and pretended she was Natalie Wood."

He also didn't pass out.

Well, Annie's just getting down to business when who walks into the Brooklyn Paramount but Joe "Joey Notches" Santucci and a couple of his gorillas, Cockeye Pastorini and Mickey "Cupcakes" LaRusso, real hard-asses in a neighborhood full of hard-asses. You think I'm bullshitting? Canarsie was so tough back in those days, our high school newspaper had a fuckin' obituary page. Recess was for evacuating the wounded.

Mickey got his name because he was crazy for Hostess cupcakes, ate fifty of 'em a day. He was a dentist's dream, with half his teeth missing. When he smiled his tongue looked like it was in fuckin' prison. What was worse, he was jealous of anyone who had more teeth than he did, which was just about everybody in Canarsie. Not a problem for Mickey Cupcakes, though—he'd just walk up and smash you in the mouth so fuckin' hard you'd be shitting molars for a month.

Cockeye Pastorini was, like, one of the scariest-looking fuckin' mugs in Brooklyn, which is no easy deal, believe me. His left eye was always half shut and his right bounced around in the socket like a fuckin' pinball, making it tough to tell if he was talking to you or the guy next to you. Cockeye was what today they call an "underachiever." At the age of nine, he set the all-time record for being the youngest kid ever booted out of P.S. 171, something to do with Cockeye pushing the teacher, Miss Toffelmeyer, out the third-floor window.

Joey Notches had just gotten his button like a week before and was now a made guy with a very well-known Mafia family, a real rising star. Not somebody you wanted to fuck with. He got his mob nickname on account of every time he whacked someone, the crazy bastard would carve a two-inch notch in his left arm. Now, some folks I know might think cutting bloody gashes in your own fuckin' arm was taking the job a little too seriously, but that was Joey Notches. When he wore long-sleeved shirts in the middle of fuckin' August, you knew he'd just capped somebody's ass.

So Joey Notches, Mickey Cupcakes, and Cockeye Pastorini take three seats in the row directly under the balcony. Right above them, Hand-job Annie's working her magic on Sammy the Shmeckle's *shmeckle*. Of course there's no way either one of them could've known who was sitting directly under them watching Dean Martin trying to get Lana Turner into the sack. Mickey Cupcakes is unwrapping a package of Hostess cupcakes; Joey Notches ain't eating anything because he had the trots the day before. Cockeye is munching on some hot buttered popcorn.

Up and down, up and down Annie's stroking Sammy's rod. He's making little grunty noises of pleasure so she knows he's about to come. Experienced cock jockey that she is, she knows to point his *shvantz* away from her, if she doesn't want to get a faceful of joy juice.

"*Oy gevalt!*" Sammy cries out, and erupts like fuckin' Krakatoa. A huge glob of baby batter jettisons straight up and sails over the balcony railing in a graceful arc, and lands flat on top of Joey's head.

Now, I don't know much about physics or any of that scientific shit, but as someone who did a little book-making, I got to say the odds of this happening are about 250,000 to one.

Up in the balcony, Sammy and Hand-job Annie hear someone, probably Joey Notches, cry out, "What the *fuck*!?"

His first thought is that a pigeon got into the fuckin' theater and crapped on his head. He dabs his finger in his hair and feels something sticky. It ain't pigeon shit. Or soda. Or even spit, he's beginning to realize with some alarm.

"Son of a bitch!" Cockeye says next as some of Sammy's load plops into his popcorn.

Only Mickey Cupcakes is spared. "What?" he asks. "What the fuck is goin' on?" He's been concentrating on the movie. They missed the first twenty minutes so he's naturally trying to catch up with the plot.

"Someone jizzed on me!" Joey Notches says indignantly, and looks up. It could only have come from above.

Back then, it was hard to imagine anyone's being crude enough to choke their chicken in a movie theater. Of course, this is still a few years before all them X-rated porno joints started popping up all over the city and guys were whacking off to *Deep Throat* and the floors were sticky enough to pull the soles right off your fuckin' Buster Browns.

Joey Notches stands up and looks up at the balcony. Even with the movie showing, it's still too dark to see anyone. He shouts, "You fuckin' piece of dirt—I'm gonna blow your fuckin' head off, you prevert!"

"Holy shit," Hand-job Annie says. "That sounds like Joey Notches. Let's get the hell out of here—he'll kill us both." And he would.

Sammy quick tries to stuff his sausage back into his pants and gets his balls caught in his zipper. Annie grabs his arm and hauls him away through a side exit door. They run down the fire escape. For Sammy, each step is a new adventure in agony.

Joey stomps up the aisle to the lobby and takes the steps three at a time up to the balcony, Cockeye and Mickey Cupcakes right behind him. Joey's beyond pissed—he's gonna personally strangle whoever did this and wasted a good haircut he'd gotten that very morning.

They get up there and the place is deserted except for old Windy McCafferty the piss bum, sleeping one off. Joey knows McCafferty probably hasn't gotten a stiff dick in years but he ain't thinking too straight at this point, so he and Mickey and Cockeye kick the shit out of Windy anyway, out of sheer frustration.

Sammy and Hand-job Annie get down to the street (Sammy's freed up his testicles by this time) and they go their separate ways, but not before Annie says to him, "You won't tell anyone about this, sport, if you wanna keep living."

Sammy doesn't need any convincing. He knows all about Joey Notches.

A few days go by and Joey Notches never does find out who jizzed on him. He lets it be known around the neighborhood that he's willing to pay a hundred dollars to anyone who might have some information. Joey's a made guy, and made guys aren't supposed to get baby batter splattered on their head. It makes him look bad.

Then one night in McTweedie's Bar and Grill, Sneed Hearn the bartender asks old Windy McCafferty why he's all beaten up. McCafferty says, "'Twas that Italian reprobate Joey Santucci and his gorillas. Someone shot their wad off the balcony and they tought it was me. Like I'd ever do anything that revoltin'."

"Yeah, I tink I heard about that," Sneed Hearn says. "I've no love for that dago bastard Joey Santucci, but I got to admit the whole affair is pretty disgustin'. Any idea who might've done it?"

Windy McCafferty says, "I'm not certain, but I thought I saw Ann Marie Hanratty in the front row with some man."

"Hand-job Annie?" Sneed Hearn asks. "That would make sense then, wouldn't it?"

He pours Windy a double Hennessey on the house and walks off to call the Sons of Garibaldi social club where Joey Notches hangs out. Sneed Hearn drops a dime. Who couldn't use a hundred dollars?

The next morning, Joey Notches and his boys pay Annie a visit at Doc Bindelbender's office. They lock Bindelbender in a closet and Annie's on the verge of a close encounter with a scalpel—Joey threatens to cut her fingers and put her out of business—and she gives up Sammy the Shmeckle as the jizz-shooter.

Joey and his boys catch Sammy on the corner of Flatbush and Avenue U.

"You had a good time with your cock, now say goodbye to your cock," Joey says as Mickey Cupcakes and Cockeye try to hold Sammy down. There's blood in Joey's eyes—he's become the fucking laughingstock of Canarsie and it's all this little Jewboy's fault. Joey's still got Bindelbender's scalpel and he has every intention of separating Sammy from his *shmeckle*. Joey and his boys played rough.

Joey says, "You think your fuckin' rabbi chopped a lot off your peepee? Wait'll you see what I'm gonna remove." What they don't realize is, even guys as small as Sammy are capable of just about anything when they think their

Chin's Chinese Restaurant, where Sammy the Schmeckle threw Mickey Cupcakes through the plateglass window. (Photo courtesy Brian Merlis, www.brooklynpix.com)

willies are on the line. Using strength he never knew he had, Sammy caught Cockeye off guard with a perfect left hook to the jaw, dropping him on the spot. Then he somehow ended up throwing Mickey Cupcakes through the front window of Chin's Chinese Restaurant, which is a pretty goddam tight squeeze. When Joey came at him, Sammy kicked the bastard hard in the gut and left him rolling around in the gutter, wailing in agony.

In our world, hitting a made guy like Joey Notches was as good as signing your own fuckin' death certificate. Joey Notches might have been crazy but, as the saying goes, he wasn't stupid. He knew good manpower when he saw it. He ended up giving Sammy a pass on both the baby-batter-on-the-head and for roughing up his crew. (Mickey Cupcakes ended up with thirty stitches in his scalp. Not from the shattered glass but from Mr. Chin's wife braining him with a cast-iron frying pan for breaking their window.)

He put Sammy to work making tribute collections and leaning on guys who were delinquent with loan-sharking payments. Sammy became a one-man collection agency and was pretty good at it until his parents packed him off to some college in, like, fuckin' Kansas to get him off the mean streets of Canarsie.

As for Joey Notches, he got into his car one day to meet some guys from Junior Gavoni's crew in Brighton Beach and was never seen again. Rumor is, Joey's helping support the foundation of a high-rise apartment building on Eighty-third and Madison Avenue.

And so it was. What the fuck—some stories *do* have a happy ending.

2. Advice from the Big Man

You know, the Big Man gets a buttload of e-mails a day from all over the world. A lot of them write to tell me how much they love my Web site and the way I can talk all kinds of shit about stuff that pisses me off. A lotta good people out there agree with the Big Man but everything's so fuckin' politically correct today people are afraid to open their yaps.

Shit, tell a fag joke and you get every fudgepacker in Greenwich Village picketing outside your house.

Tell a fuckin' lesbian joke and that fat Rosie O'Donnell and her gang of jackbooted bull-dyke buddies will cut your *shmeckle* off.

Tell an Arab joke and you got a billion fuckin' Muslim towelheads bringing a fuckin' jihad down on your ass.

Tell a Jewish joke and you get every lawyer in the fuckin' Manhattan Yellow Pages threatening to sue.

You can't even tell fuckin' Polack jokes anymore, like the one about the Polish couple who get married. On their wedding night, the husband, a virgin, is too fuckin' dumb to know what to do. So his wife tells him, "For God's sake, just take that thing you play with and stick it where I pee." So what does Polack do? He gets his bowling ball and puts it in the fuckin' sink.

Out of them 1,500 e-mails the Big Man gets each day, maybe two of them are from assholes who find me offensive. Fuck you if you can't take a joke. People like me because I say what's on my mind and don't pull no punches. My attitude is, fuck you in the ear if you're offended. You don't like what the Big Man's got to say, then don't go to my fuckin' Web site. You want nice, go watch fuckin' *Oprah* and quit e-mailing and saying I'm gonna burn in Hell when I die for all my dirty language and shit. (And if the Big Man does end up in fuckin' Hell, the first thing I'll do is kick Satan's ass and run the outfit myself.)

What's interesting, though, is that a lot of people out there e-mail me and ask for my advice on all kinds of shit. And I got to speak the truth—I'm flattered people trust me enough to ask my opinion about their personal problems. I ain't saying I'm Dear fuckin' Abby but, believe me, you could get a hell of a lot worse cause I been around awhile and I know stuff.

But I'm warning you now—you come to the Big Man for advice, it ain't always pretty. Here's a few examples:

From: FreddieG@xxxx.com
To: BigMike@TheKidFromBrooklyn.com

Dear Mr. Big Man,

I work in a small office, with maybe thirty people. There's this one guy named Julius who works in the cubicle next to mine. If I call my girlfriend on the phone, or come in two minutes late in the morning or from lunch, he rats me out to the supervisor, who comes and yells at me and threatens to fire me. How do I handle this guy?

Thanks,
Freddie in Florida

My response:

To: FreddieG@xxxx.com
From: BigMike@TheKidFromBrooklyn.com

Dear Freddie,

The only thing worse than a rat is a fuckin' office rat. You know, those sacks of shit who try to make their own sorry asses look better by making yours look bad. One time, when I was about eighteen, I was working over at DeDominico's Auto Supply over there on Flatbush Ave. And there was this guy named Vinnie who pulled the same shit on me, always ratting me out to Mr. DeDominico whenever I fucked up even just a little bit. And this Vinnie, he's a skinny little weasel-faced cocksucker. So one day I follow him into the men's room, you know, and I grab him by the shirt collar and I slap the piss out of him. I say, "You rat me out again to DeDominico, I'm gonna shove your fuckin' head into that toilet over there and keep flushing until you're floating face down in the fuckin' East River."

The little rat bastard almost shit his pants.

Now you just might be asking, did Vinnie go to the boss and get me fired for what I done? Fuck no, 'cause I also said to him, "And don't even think about going crying to DeDominico about this or I'll come to your house and cut your fuckin' balls off and feed 'em to my dog."

I didn't have no problems with Vinnie after that. I also quit that crappy job a week later because

DeDominico wouldn't give me a 25-fuckin'-cents-an-hour raise, the cheap prick.

So my advice to you is, kick the bastard's ass six ways from Sunday, or pay somebody bigger than you to do it. I see you live in Florida. I got a friend down in Fort Lauderdale who could help you out for a few hundred.

—The Big Man

Then there was this one:

From: FatTommy36@verizon.net
To: BigMike@TheKidFromBrooklyn.com

Hey, Kid,

Like you, I'm kind of overweight. Okay, I'm fat. I weigh 453 pounds. My doctor says swimming is a great form of exercise and I should join a health club that has a pool. What do you think?

—Fat Tommy in New Brunswick, NJ

My response:

To: FatTommy36@verizon.net
From: BigMike@TheKidFromBrooklyn.com

Hey Fat Tommy,

Doctors are full of shit. Swimming won't make you thin. What the fuck—you ever seen a skinny whale?

—The Big Man

3. Petey Poopie-Pants

If you didn't think the world was coming to a fucking end before, the Big Man saw a story in the newspapers about a twelve-year-old girl in some small Pennsylvania town who wet her panties in class. So what's the big fuckin' deal about that, you ask? Well, the principal of the fuckin' school called the cops—and the poor kid was charged with disorderly conduct! Can you believe this shit? What's next? We gonna start putting kids in Rikers Island for burping in algebra class?

What the fuck is going on in this country, for Chrissake? A kid pisses her pants and the dumb-ass principal calls the cops? He said that the kid had a disciplinary problem and pissed herself just to piss him off. (Talk about a pissing contest.) The girl's mother said her kid was afraid of the asshole principal. Whatever—send the kid home, don't bring in the fuckin' cops! Can you hear some police dispatcher going, "One Adam-12, one Adam-12—see the girl in sixth grade who pissed her panties. Proceed with caution—she's dripping piss on the floor and is considered wet and dangerous."

Let me tell ya, times sure have changed. When I was a kid back at P.S. 171 in Brooklyn, if you got out of line, the teacher would smack you over the head with a pointer. One time, Miss Toffelmeyer caught me chewing some Juicy Fruit in class. Did she call the cops? Fuck no—she made me put the gum on my nose and stand in front of the whole fuckin' class for an hour. Let me tell you, I never chewed no Juicy Fruit again in her classroom. A teacher tries a stunt like that nowadays and she gets fired and the school gets sued.

That's our schoolteacher, Mrs. Tofflemeyer, over on the left. She was one tough old bird. If you got out of line, she'd whack you on the head with her pointer. I still got a lump on my noggin to prove it. (Photo courtesy Brian Merlis, www.brooklynpix.com)

I remember one time, they served Yankee bean soup for lunch in the cafeteria. I don't know what the fuck they put in that soup, but it went through you faster than shit through a fuckin' goose. Jesus, we'd fart our brains out and stink up that classroom something awful. Miss Toffelmeyer used to keep a fuckin' gas mask in her desk whenever Yankee bean soup was on the lunch menu.

So a pal of mine, Petey Salerno who sat in front of me, lifted his left ass cheek to let one out. You know how it is, farting in public. You hope it's an SBD—Silent But Deadly—but sometimes your ass don't always cooperate.

So Petey lets it rip and it sounded like someone blowing a fuckin' trombone.

And if that wasn't bad enough, poor Petey under-estimated his own asshole and ended up crapping into his BVDs. So now he's got a major problem. It's only one-thirty—he can sit in his own shit until school lets out at three, or he can go public and tell Miss Tof-felmeyer the whole story. Anyone with an ounce of fuckin' pride would've just sat there and taken it like a man. Problem was, Petey was wearing white pants that day so it wasn't long before his secret leaked out.

Well, old Miss Toffelmeyer was a tough old bird—teachers were real hard-asses back then—but she could be real understanding when stuff like this happened. She told Petey to go home and get himself cleaned up. He walked out of that classroom backward so no one could see the racing stripes on the seat of his white pants. From that day on, we called him Petey Poopie-Pants.

And to this day, whenever I hear the expression "shit happens," I think of Petey Poopie-Pants.

4. The Kid's Rules for Men

I. We Ain't Fucking Mindreaders

You got a beef with something we men do, fucking *tell us* instead of moping around and trying to make us guess what's pissing you off! We ain't got time for Twenty Ques-tions like, are you mad 'cause I said your mother's apart-

ment in Bayonne smells like old farts? 'Cause I got skid
marks on your new towels? 'Cause I ate the last cannoli
you were saving for *Desperate Housewives*?

Hey, ladies—you got a wild hair up your ass for whatever reason, no problem. Women always get mad at their
husband or boyfriend—shit, it's what they do best. And
I got to admit us guys give you broads plenty to get pissed
off about. But for Chrissake, at least have the fucking de-
cency to tell us what we done to get you all bitchy.

If we ask what's wrong and you say, "Nothing," then
of course we're gonna act like nothing's wrong. What
else can we do? Hell, we know you're lying but it ain't
worth the hassle of trying to worm it out of you. Like
Scrappy Bernstein at the candy store used to say, "Never
try to teach a pig how to sing. It wastes your time and
annoys the fuck out of the pig."

II. The Toilet Seat Goes Two Ways: Up and Down

Okay, ladies, chew this one over: If we men leave the toilet seat up, why not try putting it down instead of busting our fucking balls about leaving it up? Just in case you
ain't noticed before, women squat when they go Number
One and men got to stand. We need it up, you need it
down. Shit, you don't hear us squawking when you leave
it down, so don't squawk at us for leaving it up. *Capisce?*

III. If You Think You're Fat, You Probably Are

Does this dress make me look fat? Do these pants make
my ass look too big?

Odds are, if you're asking if that dress makes you look fat, you already look like a runaway float in the fucking Macy's Thanksgiving Day Parade. Is your ass too big? If it gets into a room an hour after you do, then yeah, your ass is probably too fucking big.

Point is, ladies, you already know the answer even before you ask the question. You just want us men to convince you that you ain't fat or your ass ain't too big. Which, I got to tell you, is exactly what we're gonna fucking say if we value our peace of mind. So the next time you're trying to squeeze your size twelve ass into a size six pair of Levi's, you can expect us to say, "No, honey, you ain't fat. You look exactly the same as the day we met" and not "Yeah, you're a fucking blimp. Now go get me a beer, Elephant Woman."

5. The N Word

You know, the Big Man is really steamed about making the use of the n word illegal. For one thing, how the fuck do you enforce a law like that? What, they gonna send out the N-Word Police all over New York?

"Okay, Muldoon, N-Word Squad. Up against the wall, asshole. I'm charging you with one count of using the n word and two counts of using the f word. You have the right to remain silent . . . any use of the n word will held against you . . ."

It's just more of that political correctness bullshit from the government—the fuckers ain't content to tax our asses to death . . . now those cocksuckers who run the country want to control what we say and think, for Chrissake! Like that hate crimes bill they're trying to pass—PC dog shit.

Well, the Big Man is fucking sick and tired of the government's being up my ass all the time, so to you people I'd like to say this:

NIGGER
SPICK
KIKE
HEBE
WOP
GREASEBALL
SHEENEY
MICK
JUNGLE BUNNY
CAMEL JOCKEY
GOAT HUMPER
WHITE CRACKER
CHINK
GOOK
SLANT-EYES
DUMB POLACK
KRAUT
ACE OF SPADES
BAGEL SNAPPER
WETBACK

BEANER

RAGHEAD

BOOGIE

BORDER BANDIT

FENCE HOPPER

GOOMBAH

GHETTO MONKEY

PORCH MONKEY

REDSKIN

TACO BENDER

ZIPPERHEAD

How do you like that, you government whore cock-suckers? The Big Man will say whatever the fuck he wants, so go fuck yourself! You hear me? Go fuck yourself!

Wake up, America! Political correctness is nothing but fuckin' mind control! Say what you want, whenever you fuckin' want! Don't let these diversity bastards win!

Anyway, think about it.

6. KFC—Kentucky Fried Critters

To give you all some idea how fucked up New York City is, you don't gotta look any further than one of them Kentucky Fried Chicken places down there in Greenwich Village.

Most of them KFCs are shitholes to begin with. I mean, I change the oil in my fuckin' car every 3,000 fuckin' miles. At that fuckin' KFC, they change their cooking oil every 6,000 meals.

So it turns out the fuckin' joint was crawling with rats bigger than fuckin' Lassie, eatin' shit off the floor and dropping them huge rat turds everywhere. There was two months' worth of rotting garbage in the back. Shit, the place was filthier than a Porta-Potty at a fuckin' Ludacris concert.

So a health inspector walks in there and gives the place a passing fuckin' grade—cites 'em for a couple of nothing violations while a fuckin' rat's crawling up his leg. I bet that KFC manager was payin' off the health department, 'cause there ain't any other fuckin' explanation.

Now, if them rats were smokin' a cigarette or eatin' any trans fat on the fuckin' floor, those *gavones* at the health department would've shut the place down tighter than a virgin's twat. Those do-gooder assholes in New York wanna make you think they know what's best for you. Bake a cake with real butter and they're ready to shut your ass down. Let a fuckin' KFC turn into a petting zoo for rats, it's business as usual.

I take an oath on my mother—you wouldn't catch the Big Man eating at any KFC. For all I know, some of them rats might've ended up in that fuckin' deep fryer and served up with a side of cole slaw and some fuckin' tater tots. Jesus, that old Colonel Sanders must be spinning in his fuckin' grave.

Jesus fuckin' H Christ—stay away from them fast-food joints. First Taco Bell poisons half the country with their stinking lettuce, now KFC is puttin' ratburgers on the fuckin' menu. Eat at home, New York. The stomach you save may be your own.

Anyway, think about it.

7. The Food Nazis Strike Again

So the Big Man is pissed off. I was reading where another bunch of fuckin' do-gooder shitheads are coming down on Chinese food—saying it has a lot of fat and salt and shit and that it ain't good for you.

Some outfit called THE CENTER FOR SCIENCE IN THE PUBLIC INTEREST is sayin' Chinese food is bad for your blood pressure and your heart. The outfit sounds like it's a bunch of fuckin' feminist commie pinko bull dykes.

Jesus, Joseph, and Mary, when's the fuckin' government gonna stop sticking their big noses into every fuckin' detail of our lives? First that asshole Bloomberg puts a ban on trans fat, now they're going after fuckin' Chinese food! What's next? They gonna ban fuckin' pizza? Pastrami sandwiches? Cheeseburgers? Meat loaf? I tell ya, the world's comin' to a fuckin' end.

Take it from the Big Man—if Chinese food has so much fat in it, how come you're hungry again a fuckin' hour after you eat it?

The Big Man can't live without his Chinese food. When I was growing up in Brooklyn, there were Chinese restaurants on almost every fuckin' block—going out for Chinese on Sunday nights was what people did

back then. We used to go to a joint called the Shang-
hai Gardens. Wonton soup, chicken chow mein, pork fried
rice, an egg roll, and for dessert they'd give you a scoop
of chocolate or pistachio ice cream, all for a buck and
a quarter.

I take on oath to my mother, the fuckin' government's
turning into a bunch of fuckin' food fascists, trying to
tell us what we can eat and what we can't. To which the
Big Man says, stick it up your fuckin' ass! In a democ-
racy, it's my God-given right to eat moo goo gai pan
whenever the fuck I feel like it. I'm fuckin' sick and tired
of these socialist cunts telling us what to eat and how
to raise our kids and shit.

Stay outta my life, all you fuckin' do-gooder fatheads!
If I wanna eat a dozen egg rolls or a ton of General
Chow's chicken, that's my fuckin' business, not yours.
Stick it up your skinny stir-fried asses! Mark my words—
today Chinese food, tomorrow they'll be going after Italian food and Mexican food and steak and lobster. These
government whores won't be happy until we're all mis-
erable.

Maybe Chinese food ain't healthy but I'll tell you this:
I don't see too many fat Chinks.

Anyway, think about it.

8. Vote for the Kid in 2008

So Hillary Clinton is taking a shot at the White House
after all the bullshit about serving out her second fucking

term in the Senate. What, like you're so fucking surprised? Like you can believe one fuckin' word that comes out her wrinkled mouth? Lying is what them fuckin' Clintons do best.

Shit, old hatchet face can't even keep her fuckin' husband at home at night, he's out chasing pussy. This is who America wants in the fuckin' White House? Hillary fuckin' Clinton?

God help us if she wins—the first thing she's gonna do is go out and hire all her bull-dyke buddies for important Washington jobs. Hey—does anyone remember that fuckin' alligator wrestler Janet Reno? Do I got to say more?

Hillary in the fuckin' White House is like putting Willie Sutton in charge of security at Citibank. The Big Man thinks all the candidates, fuckin' Democrats and the fuckin' Republicans, are a bunch of fuckin' pussies. So the Big Man's decided to be the next president of these here United fuckin' States.

I'm forming an exploratory committee, whatever the fuck that is, and then I'm gonna go on a listening tour all over Jersey. And when the Big Man speaks, you better fuckin' listen.

I'm gonna get Fat Louie the bookie from the old neighborhood for my campaign manager. He's fuckin' ninety now but don't fuckin' kid yourself—he can still shatter bones with a fuckin' tire iron.

The Big Man is gonna run on the Go Fuck Yourself platform. Anyone gets in my face, I tell 'em GO FUCK YOURSELF.

The Big Man gets elected, the first thing I'm gonna

do is make all the fuckin' Starbucks charge a dime for coffee and a nickel for fresh pound cake. And no fuckin' tip cups. Fuck 'em.

Then I'm gonna build a fuckin' border fence from Texas to fuckin' San Diego that's gonna make the Great Wall of China look like a fuckin' pimple.

Then I bomb the shit out of them fuckin' Islam-o-Nazis in fuckin' Iran and Syria, get rid of that fuckin' Hezbollah. And while I'm at it, I'm gonna take care of that pain-in-the-ass fuckface Chávez down in Venezuela, the cocky little greaseball. I'm gonna send a very good hit man from Queens down there to clip the bastard.

Then I clean out the fuckin' cesspool State Department, and no more student visas for anyone named Mohammed.

So vote for the Big Man in 2008. Put some balls back into the Oval Office!

9. Horny Teachers

Well, the world's coming to a fuckin' end again today. The Big Man read where those politically correct shitheads at the New York Board of Education plan to open an Arabic school dedicated to Arabic language and culture. I used to say, only in New York, but that don't cut it anymore. This shit's happening everywhere in America.

In a pig's ass—it's fucking Muslim culture, for Chrissake! Calling it Arabic is a crock of shit, a dodge the Board of Ed is using so people don't start protesting. But the Big Man knows better.

And who's gonna pay for this Islamic school? That's right—you are, Mr. and Mrs. Sucker Taxpayer. Don't we get a say how our fuckin' tax dollars are spent? Fuck no— though I wouldn't be surprised if the fuckin' Saudi scumbags are bankrolling a chunk of this school to spread their evil Islamic bullshit in the U.S. of A.

Jesus Christ on a fuckin' crutch—no wonder everyone is fuckin' home-schoolin' their kids. I mean, you don't know what kinda PC multicultured baloney these fuckin' wack-job teachers are pumpin' into their little brains. Like Honest Abe Lincoln was a closet fudgepacker and Thomas Jefferson used to bang little black girls and America's a fuckin' racist country and the rest of the fuckin' world hates us, that kind of slop.

Anyway, what's with all this shit about female teachers fucking their fourteen-year-old boy students? Every time the Big Man opens the fuckin' paper, the science teacher is caught with a kid's pecker in her mouth or Miss Jones of Shitsville Junior High was knocked up by some squirt who doesn't even have fuzz on his little balls.

Hey, the Big Man's jealous. Shit, we didn't have any of that kind of action when I was in fuckin' junior high. Not that you'd want to, with the fuckin' horror shows we had for teachers back then. Jesus, what a bunch of fuckin' hags. There was Mrs. Bertoolis the history teacher— Beansie Harrigan said it best: "You could throw Bertoolis into fuckin' Sheepshead Bay and skim ugly for a fuckin' month."

The best-looking one was the English teacher,

Miss Tofflemeyer, and she looked like two hundred pounds of fuckin' Wiener schnitzel in a black dress. No guy who wasn't blind in both eyes wanted to see old Fatso Toffelmeyer naked. Fuck, I don't think gettin' into our pants ever crossed her mind. For one thing, teachers didn't do shit like that back then and, for another, Miss Toffelmeyer didn't have the energy. With fifty fuckin' wiseguy-wannabes like us peckerheads, we kept the old girl busier than a set of jumper cables at a fuckin' Puerto Rican wedding.

So if any of you pretty young teachers out there wanna really learn some hot stuff they didn't teach at NY fucking U, come see the Kid from Brooklyn. Just don't tell my wife, Mona.

Anyway, think about it. Or fuckin' don't.

10. I Hate Fuckin' Cell Phones

You know, the Big Man was over at the shopping mall over here in Edgewater, New Jersey, the other day. Had to go over to one of them Wal-Mart stores to get a new pair of sneakers 'cause my old pair fell the fuck apart after, like, a month, the cheap pieces of shit. Fuckin' Wal-Mart, everything they sell in that joint is made in fuckin' China or Taiwan and none of it's made to last more than ten fuckin' minutes. Time was, when you saw something marked "Made in Japan," you at least knew it was gonna be crap. The same goes now for all of them other places like Taiwan and Hong Kong. The Big Man bought a pair of pants at one of them Wal-Marts a while back and they split down the fuckin' middle before I could even get them pulled up over my ass. That's because those cock-suckin' chiselers who run Wal-Mart and them other discount joints pay those scrawny little Chinamen like twelve cents a day, which barely keeps 'em in rice and a little cooked cocker spaniel.

(Hey, the Big Man read once where they eat dogs in China. North Korea, too, 'cause that sawed-off, four-eyed midget cocksucker Kim Jung starves his people so bad they got to eat their pets. Then they all move here and the next day little Fluffy ends up a fuckin' stew pot. No shit, the truck from the Humane Society comes around and the Asians over there in Fort Lee start drooling. They call it Meals on Wheels.)

Anyway, the Big Man's walking back to his car in the parking lot wearing those crapola sneakers from Target and this big fuckin' Ford Explorer comes tearing around the corner doing a good forty miles an hour and whizzes by me—another half inch and the sideview mirror would've taken my fuckin' head off.

The Big Man catches a look at the driver—one of them pain-in-the-ass soccer moms with a couple of ankle-biters screaming in the backseat. And here's a fuckin' shock: the bitch is jabbering on one of them fuckin' cell phones with one hand and driving with the other. She whips into a parking space—no, make that two fuckin' parking spaces. She's not only fuckin' blind, she can't park for shit.

So the Big Man goes up and bangs on her window. She's still running her mouth faster than a Snapper snow-blower into that fuckin' cell phone. She rolls the window down—your typical dumbass Jersey rich broad, not half bad, looked a little like Connie Francis. They grow 'em by the truckload out here. Probably humping half the guys in town while hubby's slavin' his ass off in Manhattan and working on his first heart attack. So she says into the cell, "Hold on, Amanda, some crazy old fat man is screaming at me." Then she's got the fuckin' nerve to say to me, the snot-nosed bitch, "Excuse me, can't you see I'm talking? What do you want?"

I'm plenty steamed at this point so I say, "I need to borrow your cell phone."

I don't wait for an answer. I grab the cell phone out of her hand and say into it, "She'll call you back, Amanda, go fuck a duck." Then I fling it across the fuckin' lot, where it lands in one of them handicapped spaces and shatters into a dozen fuckin' pieces. Then I say, "If you're gonna drive one of these fuckin' Darth Vader death machines, stay off the fuckin' phone. You know you came a cunt's hair away from killin' me?"

She's so shocked her yap is hanging open like a fuckin' flounder on the hook. Not for long, though—these soccer moms ain't never at a loss for words—and she says, "You had no right to do that. I'm calling the police right now!"

"Callin' 'em with *what*?" I wanna know, and point to her busted-up cell phone. I turn to leave, then add, "And I didn't much like you callin' me fat." I can see in the backseat, two little double-chinned chubs, both girls, fightin' over a bag of Dunkin' Donuts. "Them kids of yours ain't exactly no Lindsey fuckin' Lohans. They eat any more donuts, you'll be takin' them to school in a fuckin' dump truck."

I tell you, the world's coming to a fuckin' end. Everybody and their fuckin' sister is on fuckin' cell phones all the time. What's so important it can't wait five fuckin' minutes? You wanna talk on the phone, do it in the goddamn privacy of your house, not behind the wheel of a car, for Chrissake. Shit, it's hard enough stayin' alive driving in Jersey—if you're concentrating on a fuckin' cell phone then you ain't concentrating on the road. And it's my ass that ends up in the fuckin' emergency room.

Shit, the same day the Big Man is waitin' for an elevator and right next to me is this fuckin' hump in a three-piece Brooks Brothers suit toting one of them fancy briefcases in one hand and a cell phone in the other, talking to some asshole at the top of his fuckin' lungs. He's goin', "Yes, well, Courtney and I talked about renting a villa in Tuscany this year, but she really has her heart set on Southhampton and it's just such a difficult decision since it's Jennifer's last summer before she goes off to Harvard . . ."

The elevator door opens and this shitbird don't miss a beat, still flappin' his fuckin' tongue, and now he's getting even louder. "Can you hear me? Can you hear me? I'm in the elevator." Then he has the fuckin' balls to ask me, "Would you press nineteen, please?" I say to him, "I'll press nineteen when you stick that fuckin' cell phone up your ass. And I don't give a flying fuck where you and Courtney go on fuckin' vacation." Then later when I'm comin' out of the building, some other pant-load is pushing through the revolving door and trying to dial his cell phone at the same time. The fuckin' putzhead walks around six times before the Big Man grabs him and throws his dumb ass out into the street.

The Big Man is here to tell you, put a cell phone in

some people's hands and their manners go into the fuckin' toilet. You stand on any street corner in New York City and count twenty-five people who walk by, twenty of 'em are gonna be blabbing on cell phones. And now it's even worse cause they got these fuckin' headphone things so everyone is walkin' around talking to themselves like a bunch of fuckin' zombies. The whole world's turning into *Night of the Living Dead.*

Listen up, you cell phone–lovin' son-of-a-bitch bastards—I hope them things kill all you men's sperm cells and send all you women's hormones into fuckin' hyperdrive so you can't spawn any more cell-phone usin' pantsshitters.

Anyway, think about it.

11. Tinky Vitale Gets Circumcised

The Big Man was reading today where the Board of Health is urging grown men to get circumcised cause they say it reduces the chances of gettin' the fucking HIV/AIDS virus by, like, 60 percent.

The Big Man is one of the lucky ones—I got my *shmeckle* chopped when I was a baby—it used to be a routine thing the minute you popped out of the womb. Doctor slapped your ass a couple of times and then sliced that piece of skin off the end of your little *shvantz.* But to get the peepee whacking done when you're full grown, now that's fuckin' painful.

I knew a guy in the old neighborhood in Brooklyn

named Tinky Vitale. He was the only guy in our gym class who hadn't been circumcised. Now, it ain't like us guys went around checking out other guys' peckers or nothin' homo like that, but I got to admit seeing Tinky's uncut noodle for the first time in the locker room was a real fuckin' eye-opener. It was all bunched up and shriveled looking. We started to call him Rumpleforeskin.

Then one day Tinky's excused from gym and he's walkin' around kind of hunched over like someone just kicked him in the balls. Tinky admits that a couple days before, he had to get his weewee whacked cause the foreskin was infected. He says he didn't know what the fuck pain was until the doc went at him with a scalpel.

Tinky says, "It ain't like goin' to the fuckin' barber and asking him to just take a little off the top." He admits that it's gonna take him weeks to heal up and the doc told him not to play with himself or even get a hard-on, like he'd run out of skin or something.

I mean, Jesus Christ, tellin' a seventeen-year-old kid not to get a hard-on is impossible, like trying to stuff a booger back up your nose. I mean, guys that age are fuckin' horny all the time.

Well, sadistic bastards that we were, we couldn't pass up an opportunity like this. Mikey Durso had a pack of them playing cards with a couple doing it in fifty-two different sexual positions. We jimmied open Tinky's locker and Scotch-taped them cards inside. The best one was a King of Diamonds—the couple was doing it doggie style. We didn't know that was even fuckin' possible.

Well, Tinky opens his locker and sees the cards and he can't help himself—he pops a boner right there in the fuckin' hallway and starts screaming in agony. Shit, you could hear him howling over in fuckin' Staten Island.

So the moral of the story is, if you're a grown man and the doctor says you gotta chop your doodle if you don't wanna get AIDS, then shit, get it done. But make sure you get some good painkillers and I don't mean fuckin' Advil and don't tell your pals till you heal up. Anyway, think about it.

12. The Kid from Brooklyn Q&A
Actual E-mails to the Big Man, and His Responses

Q: Dear Big Man: The other night at a party, a friend of mine got loaded and tried to squeeze my girlfriend's tit. What should I do?—Mike in Vancouver

A: What the fuck do you mean, what should you do? You should've already done it—like punching the ever-loving shit out of him or kicking him in the fuckin' balls. Now it's too late, you stupid mook. Though if he has a girlfriend, you could squeeze *her* tit.

Q: Big Man: What do you think of this Iraq war? Will it ever end? And will we win?—Raymond, Fresno, CA

A: How the fuck do I know? Who am I, General fuckin' Patton? If was up to the Big Man, we'd sell guns to both those shitty Shiites and those looney Sunnis, and let 'em put the fuckin' blast on each other. When they're done killin' each other, we'd go in and take the fuckin' oil. End of war. And, fuck yes, we'd win.

Q: Hey Big Man: My boyfriend wants to have a three-some with me and one of my girlfriends. Should I do it?—Nancy in Cleveland

A: Hey, Nancy, I been to Cleveland and there's nothing to do there. So you might as well go ahead and have the threesome. And remember to take pictures 'cause, someday, all you're gonna have are your memories. You need someone to take the photos, I'm available.

Q: Hello, Big Man: What's your favorite movie?— Sherry, Las Vegas

A: Hands down, it's *Abbott and Costello Meet Frankenstein.* I mean, shit, you got Bud and Lou—I love that little cocker—fuckin' Dracula, the Wolfman, and Frankie Boy himself. It don't get any better than that. I like the Bowery Boys too—they remind me a lot of some of the jerkoffs I used to hang with.

Q: Big Man: I seem to be attracted to tall women. Is that weird?—Harry G, Boston

A: Depends on your definition of tall. Back in the old neighborhood, there was a girl named Big Verna Eickelberger, stood six foot six in her bare feet. Well,

Verna didn't like being that tall so she had an operation where doctors removed chunks of bone in each leg, making her about five foot eleven. Fine, right? Wrong. Those fuckin' moron surgeons forgot about one thing—when Big Verna got up out of bed, her arms hung down to her fuckin' knees.

Q: Dear Big Man: You talk about the old neighborhood in Brooklyn a lot. Was it really as tough as you make it out to be?—Marci from Albany

A: It was fuckin' worse. My high school was so tough, the school paper had an fuckin' obituary page. I mean, we had guys like Beansie the Ballbuster, Bobby the Baby Raper, and Vinnie "Pizzaface" Carbone. (Vinnie had the worst zit problem in Canarsie, hence his nickname. But we never called him Pizzaface to his face—that could be fatal. You know the type—greasy black hair, leather jacket, motorcycle boots. These guys would pick their teeth with fuckin' switchblades. I once saw Beansie the Ballbuster steal the hubcaps off a moving car.)

13. Talking Toilets

I tell ya, the world's coming to a fucking end. The Big Man read today that bars in New Mexico are installing talking urinals—they tell you not to drink and drive,

right there when you're taking a fucking squirt. No shit—
they got these battery-operated urinal cakes—those things
they put in the urinals that you use for target practice—
and they're good for three months. All I know is, I'd hate
to be the poor bastard who has to change them fuckin'
batteries.

Jesus Christ, used to be a fuckin' urinal was the only
place to get a little peace and quiet—now they're gonna
be talking back as soon as you start splashing.

"*Hello, this is your urinal speaking.* "

And what the fuck—any guy who's already shit-faced
and decides to take one last leak for the road ain't gonna
pay no attention to a fucking talking piss-pot. "Hello,
this is your urinal speaking—remember, never drink and
drive. And if your piss is splattering all over you, odds
are you're standing too close."

Fuck that! Now we're getting into arguments with
fuckin' urinals. What's next, fuckin' talking toilet bowls?
You sit down to take a dump and you hear, "Hello, my
name is Timmy the Talking Toilet. Remember, always
wipe from back to front. And if you must play the ass
trombone, please be considerate of the person in the next
stall. Please flush again—there's a stray turd that didn't
go down."

Or maybe the toilet plays the fuckin' "Star-Spangled

Banner" every time you fuckin' flush. The Big Man wants his toilet to be seen and not heard. I already know how to take a shit, I don't need any fuckin' instructions.

Wake up, America—today the fuckin' toilets are talking back, who knows what's next? Your coffeemaker is gonna start saying, "Hey dipshit, your coffee's ready."

Anyway, think about it.

14. Benny Friedman, the Jewish Cattle Rustler

You know, these days if you want a hamburger or a cheeseburger, you go to a McDonald's or a Burger King or one of them joints, and sometimes they even use real meat. Or so they fuckin' tell me. Today, people take meat for granted. But when I was a kid growing up in Canarsie, real beef was a luxury the Caracciolo family couldn't afford—money was tighter than Rosie O'Donnell's grip on a bag of Cheez Doodles.

My mother worked as an office cleaner in Manhattan and it was all she could do to see that the rent was paid each month. Thank God the landlord, Mr. Greenwald, was an okay guy who didn't *kvetch* too much when the rent was late. In them days, it seemed, everyone was as poor as we were. I can count on the fingers of one hand the times we had real meat for dinner. The best my mother could afford were meat scraps from Moretti's butcher store on Saratoga Avenue—a quarter would get you a pound or two, though there was always more fat and gristle than actual beef. She'd chop up the scraps, add half a loaf of stale Wonder Bread and a couple of cups of oatmeal, and make a meat loaf, though it was usually more loaf than meat.

Benny Friedman was maybe thirteen or fourteen when his family moved to Canarsie from the Lower East Side of Manhattan. He was on the short side and had a real baby face that made him look as innocent as a fuckin' altar boy. Benny was the best *goniff* (Yiddish for "thief") any of us had ever seen. Sure, we boosted a Hershey bar from the candy store now and then, or maybe an apple or two off Mr. Grippo's s fruit stand, but that was minor-league shit. Benny Friedman could walk into Woolworth's and steal half the fuckin' toy department right under the noses of the toughest store detectives. The guy was a born thief—better than any Sicilian, and they're the greatest thieves in the fuckin' world.

Okay, so what makes a successful thief? The Big Man will tell you. It ain't how much you steal or how often you steal or even the dollar value of the swag. No, the key to being a good thief is to not get fuckin' caught. And Benny *never* got fuckin' caught—he learned from the best down there on the Lower East Side, where stealing was as natural as breathing.

Then in September 1960 a Bohack supermarket opened on the corner of Rockaway Parkway and Avenue K—a big event in Canarsie. Today you got supermarkets the size of fuckin' airplane hangars, but when I was kid in Brooklyn, there was no such thing as one-stop shopping. You went to the butcher store for meat, the bakery for bread, Old Man Grippo's for your fruits and vegetables, Mendelbaum's Milk Barn for your dairy shit, and so on. The big supermarkets like Bohack changed all that.

So one day Benny's mother gives him a quarter and sends him over to Bohack to buy a quart of milk and a pound of pot cheese so she could make blintzes. Just for the hell of it—to keep in practice maybe or just because he plain fuckin' loved to steal—Benny swiped a pound of chopped meat and shoved it up there under his armpit. He paid for his stuff and strolled out of the joint just as nice as you fuckin' please.

Of course, he couldn't bring it home—it wasn't kosher for one thing—and naturally his mother would want to know where the hell he got it. His parents were real religious Jews, and stealing was a quick way to get on God's shitlist and busting them Ten Commandments he gave Moses, right up there with breaking the Sabbath or *shtupping* your neighbor's wife. So Benny was figuring on just pitching the chopped meat into the trash when he ran into a bunch of the guys. He pulled the package out from under his armpit and said, "Anybody want?"

We didn't have to ask where he got it, knowing Benny as we did. Muzzy Marcellino offered, "I'll give youse a dime."

Well, selling the chopped meat had never even crossed Benny's mind. As *goniffs* went, he was pretty generous, always sharing whatever swag he boosted. He looked at the label—a pound of chopped meat went for thirty, forty cents back then. Benny responded, "A quarter?" Muzzy offered him fifteen cents. They settled for twenty. This was our idea of fuckin' high finance.

Word got around pretty damn quick there was a new

meat bandit in town. Pretty soon all the Canarsie guys were all over Benny like fuckin' melted mozzarella on a sausage hero, like:

"Hey, Benny, my muddah give me thirty cents for stew meat. You boost it and I'll give you half the dough."

"Yo, Benny, get me five pork butts, I'll give youse a quarter apiece for the fuckers."

It ain't long before half of fuckin' Canarsie, who hadn't tasted fresh meat in months, were lining up around the block. Benny's making money hand over fuckin' fist. We started calling him Benny the Cattle Rustler.

He was getting more offers than he can handle. But Benny was smart—he never got too greedy. He'd been at it a week and knew it was just a matter of time before the Bohack manager, Eddie Bloozer, got wise and nailed him. So for the next few days Benny starts taking the subway to a different Bohack in, like, Brownsville or East Flatbush or Ocean Hill, where they didn't know him, and hit the joint there. Problem is, Benny's got plenty of competition from the local *goniffs*, and if there's one thing a good *goniff* can spot, it's another fuckin' *goniff*. Even that baby face of his couldn't keep Benny from getting his little ass kicked from one end of fuckin' Myrtle Avenue to the other . . . Life's easier working our little chunk of Canarsie, so Benny went back to working our Bohack.

Eddie Bloozer still had his eye out for Benny and he was pissed as all hell. Benny'd lifted almost $500 worth of meat and it was making Bloozer look real bad to the big bosses. They've threatened to banish him to the bowels of fuckin' Staten Island or, worse, demote him to bag boy. Now Eddie Bloozer was hot to get his mitts on Benny.

Here's me on the left buying some stolen sausages from Benny Friedman, the Jewish cattle rustler. (Photo courtesy Brian Merlis, www.brooklynpix.com)

He said to one of the stock boys, Frankie Vinci, "When I catch that little cocksucker, I'm gonna shove that shitbird's stinkin' hand through the bread slicer. Let's see how good he steals with his digits shredded into bloody chunks."

Bloozer's serious, Frankie Vinci told us, and no fuckin' mistake. "Bloozer even made Vinnie Turso sharpen the blades on the bread slicer."

Benny decided he got to start disguising himself. So he dropped in to the local Salvation Army store and bought a battered old fedora, a scuffed-up pair of size ten wing tip shoes, and overcoat five sizes too big . . . Then he had his cousin, Noodleman the tailor, sew a dozen huge fuckin' pockets inside the coat. In exchange, Benny promised to steal Noodleman a twelve-pound standing rib roast for his kid's bar mitzvah.

Benny's next stop was Woolworth's, where he bought some white shoe polish and a pair of fifty-cent reading glasses.

With the mashed-up hat, the too-large overcoat, and those clodhoppers flopping on his feet, Benny looked thirty years older. When he streaked his hair with the shoe polish and put on them cheap glasses, he could've passed for his own fuckin' grandfather. He took the added precaution of rubbing some burnt cork on his kisser to give him some stubble.

He began clipping all the Bohack discount coupons in the *Daily News* and the *New York Post* and the *Brooklyn Eagle* until he had a big, thick stack. Then he did a test run in his disguise and snatched a brisket. Nobody gave him a fuckin' second look.

Benny waited till Saturday, the busiest shopping day in the neighborhood. He was less likely to get tagged if Bohack was crowded, which it was. He shuffled into Bohack an old man and came out a fuckin' Brooklyn legend. I saw it go down—my mother sent me to the Bohack for some baked beans and hot dogs for supper—and there was Benny, pushing a fuckin' shopping cart and muttering to himself like a lot of them old cockers walking around East Ninety-fifth Street.

It was quite a show. Benny'd grab a can of Dole pineapple chunks and a can of the store brand, pretending to compare the prices, and then toss the cheaper one into the shopping cart. Up and down the aisles he went, filling the cart with crap he had no intention of buying, studying his coupons and checking prices and pretending to argue with himself. He squeezed cantaloupes and tomatoes and even had the produce man weigh out a big bunch of green grapes. Then he ordered a pound of German potato salad at the deli counter. Benny shuffled past Eddie Bloozer in the soup aisle and even had the fuckin' balls to ask him, in one of them Jewish accents you used to hear, "So maybe you could tell me vere deh prunes is at, please?"

Eddie, who looked perpetually pissed off, whizzed right by Benny, taking him for just another old pain-in-the-ass shopper. He said, "Aisle six," and charged into the stockroom, probably to rip some poor bastard a new asshole for not stacking the canned peas the right way. Eddie was a screamer. All the cashiers and stock boys hated his fuckin' guts, which didn't exactly inspire any loyalty. Shit, they didn't care if Benny or Jesus Christ himself stole the store fuckin' blind.

Benny putzed his way over to the meat department like he had all the time in the world. He checked the price on a plastic-wrapped package of beef short ribs with his left hand and stashed another inside his coat with his right—I take an oath to my mother, I've never seen nothing like it. That right mitt of his was faster than a fart in a fuckin' back draft.

Here's a list—and I remember this down to the last fuckin' link of pork sausage—of what Benny the Cattle Rustler glommed that day:

A two-pound boneless beef chuck roast (for Philly Bonnacorso)

Two lamb chops (for Butchie Buschetta)

Three pounds of minute steak (for Mickey the Mook Scalifani)

A two-and-a-half pound top round London broil (for Big Sally Rotondo)

A four-pound pork shoulder (for Dom "Baldy" Balderino)

A pound of slightly moldy pig's feet (no takers— nobody wanted to admit asking Benny to steal that shit)

A really skinny kosher chicken (for Melvin Kaminsky—"Did it touch the pork?" Melvin wanted to know. "'Cause if it did, I ain't payin'." Benny said to him, "And if my mother had balls, she'd be my father." Melvin took the bird.)

Two pounds of hamburger that was more brown than red and didn't smell too good—super- markets didn't give a rat's ass about expiration dates back then (for John "Corky" Vastola— Come to think of it, we didn't see Corky for a while after that.)

Now, you might think that walking out of a Bohack with almost twenty-five pounds of meat (which is a third of what Benny weighed) in your fuckin' pockets is easy; the Big Man is here to tell you it takes balls like co- conuts. Benny only made it look easy.

But he wasn't out of the woods yet. There were six cash registers but most times only four of them were in use, because Eddie Bloozer was such a shitty boss that the cashiers were always quitting on him. When he wasn't screaming at those gals, he was pinching their ass-cheeks. Fewer cashiers made for longer lines but that was okay with Benny—the busier the joint was, the easier it was to slip out without anyone seeing.

That Saturday, though, Benny didn't figure on five cashiers showing up. There were four working when he started—Benny preferred a minimum of two escape routes whenever possible. One of the cashiers must have come on while he was boosting the goodies. He made straight for the empty checkout lane but then Eddie Bloozer came flying out of nowhere—muttering about those dumb, lazy cunts he hired who never showed up half the fuckin' time—and manned the last register. Benny grabbed a bottle of Thousand Island salad dressing and got on another line behind some fat lady with her cart loaded halfway to the goddamn ceiling, hoping she'd block him from Eddie's view.

"Next in line," Eddie Bloozer called out, and looked straight at Benny, who was about to crawl up the fat lady's ass just to get the hell out of there. "Over here, old man. I'm open."

Benny had no choice—the aisles were packed, so there was no way he was gonna bolt. He shuffled over to Eddie's aisle like a man walking the last mile to the fuckin' hot seat. He put the salad dressing down and Eddie started punching the register, not looking up. Benny owed twenty-two cents for the Thousand Island but he had a grand total of nine cents in his pocket. He started rooting around in his baggy old-man pants, searching for twelve cents he didn't have and hoping for a miracle.

Benny was twisting around so much a package of Kahn's hotdogs (for Fuddy Featherstone) slipped out from under his armpit and dropped to the floor. Eddie Bloozer looked up from the register and now he gave Benny a cold, hard look. Benny was smothering from all the heavy clothes and started sweating his balls off—another two minutes and Corky Vastola's chopped meat would start sizzling in his crotch, where Benny had stashed it. Some of the white shoe polish started running down his forehead.

Benny was dead and he knew it. Which made him *schvitz* even worse and his face became covered with white streaks.

Now I told you, in the Bohack that day, I'd been watching Benny stealing in the finest fuckin' tradition of Sicilian thievery. He was in a real fuckin' jam—Eddie was pretty slow in the head but it was dawning on him that something wasn't right about this old geezer. Even old farts don't sweat white. Only one guy could save Benny's ass now and that was yours truly. Benny was a pal, and you always try to help out a pal when he's in the deep shit.

As it turned out, I was standing by the canned juice—there was a shelf full of Hawaiian Punch off to my right. I didn't even think about it, just swept my arm across that shelf and sent a dozen cans of that sweet shit crashing to the floor, then hoofed it to the back of the store where they kept the crap no one wanted, like Limburger cheese and SPAM. They sounded like gunshots. For a half second everyone thought it was Vito "Socko" Guardino, who did hits for Tommy Funzi, blowing the heads off chickens again for target practice in his courtyard. (A pretty sick hobby, everyone in the neighborhood agreed, but only someone with a death wish would have the balls to ask Socko to stop. Besides, after he blew their heads off, Socko gave the dead chickens away for free.)

Well, there were cans of Hawaiian Punch rolling all over aisle twelve. Eddie Bloozer went running over, cursing up a storm, Benny forgotten for the moment. The last thing Eddie needed was some pain-in-the-ass customer tripping over one of those cans and suing the pants of the whole friggin' Bohack chain.

No fool he, Benny bolted out of the joint like his pants were on fire and didn't stop running until he was halfway to Bensonhurst, leaving a trail of rib roasts and pork shoulders all over Rockaway Parkway.

Benny cleared a small fortune that day—close to forty dollars, I seem to remember, and he likely could've doubled or even tripled it the next week if he'd wanted to. But the close call with Eddie Bloozer sort of unhinged him and he decided to retire from the meat-boosting racket. In fact, I don't think Benny did much stealing at all after that Bohack caper. Seems Benny's mom was cleaning out his closet a couple of days later and found two hundred dollars rolled up in a pair of old argyle socks he never wore. Benny tried to bluster it out, claiming he found it in an alley after a crap game, but Mrs. Friedman wasn't buying it. Benny was a great *goniff* but a lousy liar. She slapped the shit out of him until he confessed, then dragged him down to the synagogue and told Rabbi Meltzer what Benny had done. Then the rabbi slapped the shit out of him. After, he told Mrs. Friedman to leave his office—he wanted to talk to Benny alone.

When she was gone, Rabbi Meltzer asked him, "Maybe you could get me a nice kosher breast of veal?"

We didn't see much of Benny after that. In fact, a month or so later, he and his family moved again, this time to Queens, Jackson Heights I think it was, and that was a long way from Canarsie. Then, about five years ago, I ran into him at Katz's Delicatessen, of all places, down there on the Lower East Side of Manhattan. Almost forty-five years later, he looked pretty much the same—he never did grow much taller than five foot five and he still had that apple-cheeked baby face. He didn't have much hair left, and what he did have was more silver than black.

We each got a corned beef sandwich and a Dr. Brown's black cherry soda, and sat down at a table. Benny said, "You know, Mike, I never did thank you."

"What the hell for?" I asked him.

"For knocking those cans of Hawaiian Punch off the shelf so I could slip out the Bohack and not get killed by Eddie Bloozer. You really saved my bacon that day, you'll pardon the expression."

"Fuggedabouddit," I said. "You woulda done the same for me."

So we ate and schmoozed about the old days back in Canarsie. Turns out Benny done okay for himself. He found a profession that was perfect for an old thief. He became a lawyer. I guess old habits die hard.

15. You Really Need the Kid in 2008!

I tell ya, the world' coming to a fucking end. The Big Man was reading in *USA Today* where known fuckin' Muslim extremists are applying for jobs as school bus drivers—and the fuckin' FBI says it's okay!

Jesus Christ, what the fuck is going on here?

We should be kicking these fuckin' cocksucking rat bastards out of this country and instead we're letting 'em drive our children to school? What the fuck is wrong with the FBI? Are they so fuckin' afraid of pissing off the very people who wanna kill us that they're gonna let them use buses to blow up New York or Chicago, instead of using airplanes?

"I'm sorry we can't let you take flying lessons, Mr. Terrorist, but here are the keys to the school bus. Please don't slaughter my little Tommy and Suzie."

The Big Man says it's time to clean house in Washington. Throw all the bums out at the fuckin' FBI and the CIA and the rest of 'em. Put the Big Man in the White House and fire each and every one of those stupid fuckin' mooks who are supposed to be protecting us. Department of Homeland Security, my big dimpled ass—if those pencil pushers in the FBI and the CIA were doing their fuckin' jobs on 9/11 like they were supposed to, we wouldn't need no department of homeland security.

First thing the big man's gonna do when he's the president is round up every fuckin' Muslim in the country and kick their asses back to whatever shithole they came from. Then the Big Man's gonna bring in his own crew to run the FBI and the CIA.

I'm gonna put Mike the Steamfitter in charge of the FBI—the guy's almost seven fuckin' feet tall and no one's gonna fuck with him. Then I'm gonna make Toothpick Charlie from Bensonhurst the head of the CIA—he'd make a great spy cause he wore a wire for the feds and helped send fifty wiseguys to the can.

Wake up, America, and vote for the Big Man in 2008. I'll take America back from the screwballs and the politically correct peckerheads who are ruining this great country. Vote for the Big Man, and put some balls back in the White House!

16. Tommy and Teresa's Sex Problem

Once upon a fuckin' time, I remember, back in the old neighborhood (Canarsie, Brooklyn, for you fuckin' idiots who didn't know. Jesus fuckin' Christ, listen to me talk—where the hell else would I be from?), everybody had a nickname. I knew a couple a nice kids from Ninety-fifth Street, Tommy Coletti and Teresa DeSalvo. Childhood sweethearts, started going around together from the time they was in fifth grade.

(The P.S. stands for Public School—all the elementary schools and high schools had numbers, not names, probably 'cause those lazy cocksuckers in the New York City government who were in charge of naming schools decided numbers were easier than actually having the fuckin' brains to do some homework and find some good dead person to name the school after. If they'd have asked me, I woulda suggested naming the school for Morris Goldblatt who ran Goldblatt's Kosher Deli over there on Seventy-third Avenue. Back then, they knew how to make a fuckin' great sandwich. Old Morris would stack the corned beef and pastrami so thick you could barely fit it into your yap to take a bite. I remember a local bookie named Fat Andy Petrillo—guy weighed, like, five hundred fuckin' pounds. He used to eat three of Goldblatt's chopped liver and onion sandwiches at one sitting. One day Morris said to him, "*Oy gevalt*, Andy, you eat like you got two assholes." To me, Morris Goldblatt is a true American hero. Worked in that fuckin' deli from six in the morning until ten at night—he fed three generations of people from the neighborhood. If you were a little down on your luck, he'd feed you on the cuff until you got back on your feet. I swear on my mother, he made matzo balls the size of a planet. So you'd think one of those fuckin' dumbbells in charge of school names would've honored him.)

Anyway, so Tommy and Teresa, they're only eighteen but they went ahead and tied the knot over at St. Anthony's church. You might think eighteen's a little young to get married but people grew up faster in them days. Shit, half the fuckin' kids in this country today are still living at home with Mommy and Daddy when they're thirty, the lazy cocksuckers.

Now you got to understand that kids didn't know much about sex back then. They didn't have that fuckin' porn you can get on your computer or those whores like Britney Spears or Paris fuckin' Hilton flashing their goodies all over the television and humping every guy west of the fuckin' Mississippi. In them days, you learned about sex on the street and most of what you heard was bullshit, a bunch of macho dickheads trying to impress their buddies.

So Tommy and Teresa were both virgins on their wedding night. (How do I know this? None of your fuckin' business how I know, okay? This was fuckin' Brooklyn, where people live on top of each other—there weren't any secrets.)

So a couple of years go by. Tommy had a good job over there at Kennedy Airport (it was called Idlewild Airport back then) drivin' a forklift—and, from where I sat, they seemed to be doing okay.

Except for one thing: Neither one of them was too happy with the way things were going in the fuckin' bedroom, if you know what I mean. Hey, you got to realize that Teresa was a nice Catholic girl and in them days, sex wasn't discussed the way it is today. I mean, when it came to doing the old horizontal mambo, Tommy didn't know shit and Teresa knew even less. And they were too shy and embarrassed with each other to even talk about the problem. I mean, who was Teresa gonna talk to about it? Father Anthony over at St. Bernadette's? Fuggedabouddit—Father Tony never met an altar boy he didn't love, that fudge-packing piece of shit. The nuns? Forget them—their idea of a good time was ten minutes with a fuckin' candlestick and a can of Crisco. Teresa's mother? Nice girls didn't talk to their mothers about screwing back then. So it was up to Tommy to take the situation in hand, if you know what I mean.

So one day Tommy went over to Plotkin's bookstore over on Belmont Avenue and bought one of them sex

Belmont Avenue in Brownsville, Brooklyn, where Tommy Coletti bought a book showing all kinds of sexual positions. The one Tommy tried out on his wife Teresa didn't work out too well. (Photo courtesy Brian Merlis, www.brooklynpix.com)

manuals that has all these pictures in it of all the different sex positions. It blew his fuckin' mind, too—he couldn't believe people did shit like that in the sack. (Up until then, Tommy's idea of sex was jumping on top of Teresa and badda beep, six thrusts and it's time for *Bonanza*.)

One sex thing in there called "sixty-nine" caught his eye. If you know what this is, I've got no need to explain it. And if you don't know what sixty-nine is, you dumb fuck, you ain't living right.

That night, Teresa makes a big pot of linguine and broccoli with lots of garlic and olive oil for dinner, one of Tommy's favorites. He rushes her through dinner and don't even give Teresa the chance to wash the fuckin'

dishes. He takes her hand and walks her into the bedroom, sits her down on the bed, and shows her the book
he got from Plotkin's. He flips to the page where the
people are doing sixty-nine and he says to her, "Let's
try this tonight, okay?"

Well, Teresa loves her husband very much and she knows
he's as bored with their sex life as she is, so she agrees.
They take off their clothes and crawl into bed and work
themselves into the sixty-nine position, just like the book
shows. And they're just about to get down to it when
what happens? Tommy blows a huge fart right in Teresa's
face. *Fare una puzza!* He can't help it—she used too much
fuckin' garlic in the linguine and, between that and the
broccoli, he's got enough fuckin' gas to keep all of fuckin'
Brooklyn warm for the winter.

So Tommy apologizes and they try again. And the
same thing happens—they get into the sixty-nine position and Tommy farts in her face again, even worse this
time, stinkin' up the whole fuckin' apartment. By this time,
Teresa's getting a little upset and who could blame her?
I mean, who likes having farts blown in their face?

Tommy gets up and goes into the bathroom to splash
some water on his face. He comes back to the bedroom,
hoping to try that sixty-nine thing one more time. When
he gets there, Teresa's hiding under the bed. So Tommy
says to her, "What the hell are you doing under the bed?"

And Teresa says, "If you think I'm going through that
sixty-seven more times, *vaffanculo!*" (Which means "up
your ass" in Italian.) My hand to God, this is a true story.

The moral of the story is this: If you're gonna do

sixty-nine, don't eat linguine with garlic, because it makes you play the ass trombone. *Capisce?*

Anyway, think about it.

17. Gas Attack

Some of you may have read about the situation we had here in New York recently. The smell of gas came wafting over Manhattan, down on Wall Street, all the way uptown. Buildings were fuckin' evacuated, the subways shut down, the whole ball of wax.

The Big Man's first thought was, maybe them Mexicans over there in Weehauken were having themselves a taco-eating contest. Or maybe all that gas was coming from Rosie O'Donnell.

But no—Mayor fuckin' Bloomberg says it's just gas rising from the swamps over across the river in Secaucus.

Swamp gas? Bull-fucking-shit, Bloomberg! This wasn't no swamp gas from Secaucus—yeah, go ahead, pin it on Jersey. I been to Secaucus—it's maybe seven, eight miles

If New York City survived four years of Mayor David fuckin' Dinkins, it can survive anything.

south of where I live here in Fort Lee. There ain't enough swamp down there to produce that much gas. Not to mention, how come in all the years Secaucus has been on the map this ain't happened before?

I'll fuckin' tell you why—cause it wasn't any fuckin' swamp gas. It's those fuckin' Muslim cocksucking terrorists doing a dry run for the day when they try to pull off the next fuckin' 9/11. Why don't you fuckin' tell the truth, Bloomberg? What, you think we can't handle it? Shit, if New York City survived four years of Mayor David fuckin' Dinkins, it can survive anything.

Now, the Big Man ain't one of them paranoid conspiracy cheeseheads, but sometimes you got to do the fuckin' math. I saw yesterday in Austin, Texas, a million fuckin' birds just dropped from the sky like fuckin' raindrops. And nobody fuckin' knows why. Then the same fuckin' thing happened down in Australia. And they can't fuckin' figure it out, either.

I ain't sayin' these things are connected, but who says they ain't? And when you're dealing with those fuckin' cocksuckin' Arab terrorists, it's healthy to keep an open mind. Who knows what kind of shit they could be pumping into the air to see what kind of damage it causes? Today it's birds, tomorrow it's Joe Sixpack and Mrs. Soccer Mom.

Does the Big Man sound paranoid? You bet your ass.

So open your eyes, America! Don't believe the horseshit you read in the papers. Get out there and start asking questions. Your fuckin' life may depend on it.

18. The "Go Fuck Yourself" Platform

You know the Big Man has decided to run for president in 2008. So I'm hitting the campaign trail big time. Here's the Big Man's stand on the issues.

One: If I'm elected, the first thing I'm gonna do is toss that cracker bastard Jimmy Carter into a fuckin' old-age home and make sure they pump his Georgia ass full of elephant tranquilizers so he can't go around bad-mouthing the United States and taking money from the fuckin' Arabs.

Two: I'm gonna shut down that fuckin' Council on American-Islamic Relations, that fuckin' CAIR, the fifth column bastards. Then I'm gonna shut down all the mosques and kick those bearded imans out of the country. I'm gonna turn all those fuckin' mosques into Jewish delis 'cause we have too many mosques and not nearly enough fuckin' pastrami sandwiches.

Three: I'm gonna tell the big oil companies to go fuck themselves—find some oil from a friendly country, for a fuckin' change. If we can't find a friendly country, then we find an unfriendly country with a lot of oil and bomb their asses into the middle of next week. Then we'll just take their fuckin' oil. They don't like it, they can go fuck themselves.

Four: I'm gonna make it illegal to be or even be named Rosie fuckin' O'Donnell. I'm gonna hunt her down and put a fuckin' muzzle on her big mouth and lock her in a fuckin' cage so I don't have to look at her ugly mug.

Five: I'm gonna deport the Reverends Al Sharpton and Jessie Jackson to fuckin' Somalia. 'Cause I'm fuckin' sick of both of their asses. They're always pissing and moaning how blacks are mistreated in America. You think you got it fuckin' tough here, assholes, try living in that hellhole for a while.

Six: I'm gonna shut down the fuckin' *New York Times* 'cause I'm fuckin' sick of their anti-America bullshit. Shit, no one will miss that fuckin' rag anyway.

Seven: I'm gonna send some rockets up in space and blow the shit out of Al Jazeera's fuckin' satellite. I'm sick of their fuckin' bullshit, too.

Eight: I don't give a flying fuck if those Pakis don't like it— I'm gonna send a Delta Force into that shithole country and say, "Turn over bin Laden or you're fuckin' toast, you cocksuckers."

Vote for the Big Man in 2008. Put some balls back in the White House.

19. Muslim Boycott

So the Big Man read today where a bunch of fuckin' Muslims are calling for a boycott of Northwest Airlines. Seems they were coming back from that fuckin' Muslim Woodstock over there in Mecca, and Northwest wouldn't let those goat-humpers on the plane to Detroit.

Now they want Northwest to apologize and punish their employees, and they're trying to shake down the airline for some fuckin' dough. I can't believe the balls on these raghead cocksuckers! If I was the pilot on that plane, I wouldn't let those fuckin' pricks onboard, either. Racial profiling—that's the way to go when it comes to that bunch. You don't like it, Muslims, then fuckin' walk. It was good enough for fuckin' Muhammad. Or buy yourself a fuckin' flying carpet. I don't give a shit.

So now these camel jockeys are calling on all Muslims to boycott Northwest 'cause the airline won't back down, God bless 'em. So everyone write to Northwest Airlines and tell 'em they're doing a great job. Don't let these Arab cocksuckin' terrorists intimidate us anymore.

Hey, Muslims—why don't you do us all a fuckin' favor and boycott all the fuckin' airlines. Let's make ALL air travel fuckin' Muslim free. Let 'em start their own fuckin' airline if they don't wanna be racially profiled.

And while you're at it, boycott Amtrak and the subways and the buses and the shopping malls. Hell, why don't you boycott all of America. I'm fuckin' sick of your death-to-America bullshit anyway.

Hey, Northwest—you got the Big Man's business from now on. I think the rest of the airlines should get into the No Muslim racket—their business would triple overnight!

Anyway, think about it.

20. Rotten Applebee's

You know, the Big Man and my wife, Mona, were out at the mall doing some shopping and we went into one of them fuckin' Applebee's. I can tell you this right off— the food looks a lot better on their TV commercials than it does on your fuckin' plate.

The Big Man ordered himself a steak—at least those pricks *said* it was a fuckin' steak. It was the size of my fuckin' pinkie. Then I fuckin' broke three knives tryin' to cut into it. I said to the waitress, "Hey honey, get me a fuckin' chainsaw so I can cut this fuckin' thing." It was tougher than a catcher's mitt.

Then my Mona ordered some kind of salad. The fuckin' plate looked like the bottom of a hamster's cage. And the chicken in the fuckin' salad wasn't right. I said to the waitress, "Twenty years ago, this really fat lady was climbing on to the Broadway bus and she lost her balance and fell backward and her ass went right into my face. I never smelled nothing that bad until I smelled this fuckin' chicken."

So the manager came running over, some kid looked like he was fuckin' twelve. He said, "Is anything the matter?" I said, "Fuck, yeah. You got a lotta balls charging money for this shit. *Eatin' good in the neighborhood*, my fuckin' ass. I don't know what fuckin' neighborhood you come from, but if you ever opened one of these joints in Canarsie when I was growing up, we'd have torched the shithole the first fuckin' day."

Me and Mona got the fuck out of there and went to

an Italian joint close to home, which is what we should've done to begin with. How can people eat at that fuckin' Applebee's? Stay home, America, and make a fuckin' meat loaf or some nice pasta.

Stick it up your ass, Applebee's.

21. Toilet Paper

So the Big Man was reading where that Sheryl Crow is sayin' we oughta use only one piece of fuckin' toilet paper every time we take a shit. Hey, even using both sides, one piece of toilet paper just don't cut it.

Jesus fuckin' Christ—the world's comin' to a fuckin' end. Now these Hollywood wackos wanna tell us how much toilet paper we should be usin'.

The Big Man doesn't know this Sheryl Crow except she got dumped—you'll pardon the expression—by that Lance Armstrong.

But that ain't the point. In the first place, who the fuck is any Hollywood scumbag to tell me how to wipe my ass? Second, assholes are like snowflakes—no two are the same.

Maybe this Sheryl Crow drops tiny turds like Milk Duds, but not the Big Man. When I pinch a loaf, you can hear the plop all the way to fuckin' Pittsburgh. And it takes a lot more than one piece of fuckin' toilet paper to wipe my slate clean. And I sure as hell don't want anyone keeping track of my sinkers and my floaters. Fuck—you know how thin one piece of toilet paper is? What if it breaks when you're wiping? I don't know about you, but the Big Man doesn't want to go poking himself in the ass every time he's droppin' friends off at the pool.

You know, when the Big Man was a kid back in Brooklyn, toilet paper was a real luxury. Most of the time, we used the *Daily News* or the *Brooklyn Eagle*.

The Big Man is fuckin' tired of these Hollywood liberal fuckheads telling me how to live. Shit, if I wanna wipe my butt clean with the fuckin' Pine Barrens of New Jersey, that's my business.

And hell, how would you even enforce a law like that? You'd need Turd Police to stand over you while you're sitting on the pot. What, you wipe with two pieces of toilet paper and they write you out a fuckin' ticket? I mean, give me a fuckin' break. That ain't a job I would want, havin' to listen to people playin' the ass trombone for eight hours at a fuckin' time.

What if you get the fuckin' Hershey squirts? You think one piece of paper is gonna do the trick? Maybe the Sheryl Crows of the world would be happier if we just wiped our asses with our fuckin' underpants.

And if that ain't bad enough, this crazy fuckin' Sheryl Crow says we should wipe our mouths with our sleeves at the fuckin' dinner table? Shit, the Big Man spent his whole life trying *not to* wipe his mouth with his fuckin' sleeve. In my day, this was called "good manners."

Go fuck yourself, Sheryl Crow.

22. Bat Day

Before we even get started, I've got to get this one off my chest. Here ya go: first stuffed condom out of the mule, as they say. A lot of you who know me from the Internet already know how I feel about fuckin' ballpark security.

It's gotten completely out of hand since 9/11. By the time you get in the fuckin' park, it's time to leave to beat the traffic. Take yer seat, have a twelve-dollar beer, and it's time to go. Two hours on the Major Deegan trying to get across the G.W. with the guy behind you leaning on the fuckin' horn.

A friend of mine took his kid to Yankee Stadium the other day and it took them two and a half hours to get inside the fuckin' ballpark. Two and a half fuckin' hours. Security has got to check everything. They got to check your bags. Check your pockets. They're taking away a guy's penknife. It's a fuckin' jacknife, with a fuckin' corkscrew in it for opening fucking wine bottles. It's out of hand.

And, and! In the meantime, it's fuckin' Bat Day. They're handing out fifty thousand fuckin' baseball bats! So they search everyone for weapons and then, the instant the people clear security, the guards hand them a fuckin' baseball bat. At first it seemed stupid and then I realized it was brilliant. These security guys are fuckin' geniuses.

Then, it occurs to me. The airlines should get in on this racket. We could stop all these fuckin' long security lines at the airport. New fuckin' policy. Every passenger on our planes gets a fuckin' baseball bat!

What could it cost 'em? Two, three dollars apiece

wholesale? Just add it into the cost of the fuckin' airline ticket. Everybody on the fuckin' plane has got their fist around a fuckin' Louisville Slugger.

You could play it two ways. You could let everybody keep the bat, just like on Bat Day at Yankee Stadium, or you could confiscate the bats as the passengers get off the fuckin' plane, and use the same bats again for the next flight.

If you're an A-rab cocksucker hijacker and you get on that fuckin' plane, what are you gonna do when you see two, three hundred people on the fuckin' plane with fuckin' baseball bats? You ain't gonna do fuckin' much.

You're gonna stick your finger up your ass and whistle Dixie. You gonna get the fuck out of there. And this dawned on me also: if I was a passenger of that fuckin' plane and I was on there with a baseball bat, I would love to fuckin' brain that A-rab cocksucker over the head with the baseball bat.

Bam! It would be like fuckin' Smashin' Pumpkins, an all-right band but they should lay off the smack. I'd hit the A-rab cocksucker hijacker over the head with my fuckin' baseball bat and send 'em to Blue fuckin' Heaven.

23. Trans Fat This, Fucko

As if the fuckin' government wasn't up our asses enough already, now those cockeyed shit-for-brains, do-gooder assholes wanna ban trans fat—you know, the stuff they

Here I am standing in front of Nathan's. Their hot dogs are full of trans fat. I hope you like this photo cause I froze my fuckin' balls off having it took. (Photo courtesy Kevin Helmick)

use to bake bread and cakes and cookies and White Castle hamburgers and shit like that.

You'd think after 9/11, when those cocksuckin' Arab terrorists parked a couple of jets inside the World Trade Center, those *putannas* down in Washington would have enough to keep them busy, like stopping those crazy ragheads from exploding a suitcase bomb in the middle of fuckin' Times Square or something.

But no. None of those gutless pukes we call politicians in this country got the fuckin' balls to bring the fight to those death-loving goat-humpers in Iran and Iraq and Syria.

If the Big Man were president, I'd flatten those third-world shitpiles with a couple dozen A-bombs and nuke the fuckers till they glowed in the dark. Hey, ragheads—*Andate tutti a fanculo.*

You want your seventy-two fuckin' virgins? I got your

seventy-two virgins right here. I hope they all turn out to be drag queens from Greenwich Village, you *finocchio* bastards.

So instead of knocking off our enemies and lowering taxes, those morons in D.C. wanna make using trans fat illegal. And the worst is that fuckin' mayor of New York City, that *gavone* Bloomberg, the fuckin' health nut.

First he bans smoking and now he's going after restaurants and bakeries and places that use trans fat. Everything's gonna taste like fuckin' cardboard. We let Bloomberg get away with this horseshit, what's next?

He gonna ban screwing? Or maybe just fuckin' screwing in anything but the fuckin' missionary position. Sorry, Mr. Doggie Style, the fucking Fuck Police are here to give you and your doggie wife a ticket.

Maybe he'll decide we're wasting too much fuckin' air and they'll pass some jerkoff law sayin' we can only breathe every other day.

And get this—friend of mine over here in Jersey took his eight-year-old daughter to parent-student night at the elementary school. So the school brings in some fancy-ass broad who's some sorta fuckin' expert on nutrition or some shit. She tells all the parents their kids can only have healthy snacks—raisins and yogurt and carrot sticks and so on. I mean, that's okay sometimes but, for Chrissake, whatever happened to fuckin' cookies and milk?

What, the kid eats a fuckin' Mallomar, he's gonna have a heart attack? When I was a kid, I ate Hostess cupcakes and Oreos and Hershey bars, and I'm still fuckin' alive and kicking.

I'm telling you, we're raising a whole generation of pussies. Don't get me wrong, I've got nothing against carrot sticks and yogurt—though I never cared for that crap personally. Open up one of them yogurt things, it looks like a humpback whale whacked off into a fuckin' Dixie cup.

No, what really pisses me off is the government *tellin'* us what our kids and can and can't eat. The Big Man is fucking *sick* of the government sticking their big honkers into my life. No trans fats, eh?

Let me tell you something—if I wanna shove a butt-load of cannolis down my gullet, that's my fuckin' business, not yours. If I wanna eat Big Macs and fries six times a day, who the fuck is the government to tell me I can't?

Fuck you, Washington.

Stick it up your granola-eatin' ass, Bloomberg. Fuck you too, Hitlery Clinton. You're just as bad as Bloomberg. Why don't you drop five or fifty pounds off those torpedo legs of yours? It takes a village, my ass.

Anyone can eat yogurt and bran muffins, but it takes a real man to stand up to a triple bypass.

Takes a fuckin' village to satisfy that *stronzo* husband of yours. (Though I got to say, if I had to look at you naked, I'd fuck around, too.) Bunch of fuckin' Nazis, that's who we got running the show in this country.

The Big Man ain't gonna take it. And hear this, you fucks: Anyone can eat yogurt and bran muffins, but it takes a real man to stand up to a triple bypass. Me, when it's the Big Man's time to go, mark my tombstone REST IN PIZZA, you turds.

24. Outsource This!

I tell ya, having a Web site can be a fuckin' pain in the ass. I got a tech guy, which helps a lot, but some of the shit that happens, you wouldn't fuckin' believe. Take the other day. People tried to log on and got a picture of a fuckin' Muslim crest in a waterfall.

Some piece of camel crap from Turkey hacked into the Big Man's Web site with the words "I to protest," the fuckin' illiterate. Ain't it bad enough we're outsourcing all our jobs over to these third-world shitpiles?

Now the fucks are hacking our Web sites on their fuckin' coffee breaks.

Yeah, bring it on, fuckin' Abdul, come over here to Jersey and come get your fuckin' seventy-two virgins. Fly over from that flea-infested country of yours, you want to take on the Big Man.

(Don't worry about getting searched over there at Newark Airport—fuckin' security only hassles old ladies and midgets.)

Like every good American should be, the Big Man is fed up with these filthy-rich corporations sending all their fuckin' jobs to Pakistan and Uzbekistan and Suck-my-assa-stan.

Friend of mine here on the blog bought one of them Blackberrys for his kid the other day. He was having problems, so he called the help desk and ended up talking to some hump in Bombay.

"Beedybottybiddyboop," the fuckin' guy said.

"Huh?" my friend asked.

"Beedybottybiddyboop," the guy repeated.

"Same to you, asshole," my friend said and fuckin' hung up. Then he fuckin' complained to me, "I couldn't understand a fuckin' syllable the guy said."

So he took the computer back to fuckin' Best Buy or one of them joints and said to the manager, "First, shove this fuckin' Blackberry up your blowhole, then gimme one where I can speak to a fuckin' American when I call their fuckin' help desk."

Take it from the Big Man, the world's coming to a fuckin' end. Why the fuck do we have to export jobs when we got millions of honest, hard-working Americans crying for work?

It's because these huge fuckin' corporations can pay those people over in India ten fuckin' cents a day. So the next time you call your bank or those bloodsucking vampires at Visa and MasterCard (22 percent interest, some of those fuckin' leeches charge—shit, you can get a better rate with a loanshark, for Chrissake), demand to speak to an American or else tell 'em to take their credit cards and shove 'em up their greedy fat asses, the cocksuckers.

Fuck you, Starbucks. (Photo courtesy Kevin Helmick)

25. Starbucks

The Big Man woke up the other morning and he had a craving for a good cup of coffee and a piece of pound cake. I'm over here in New Jersey, and I ended up in one of them Starbucks. You know the place? They got 'em all over the fuckin' place. About one every other block.

I knew the joint wasn't right the second I walked in. Something was hinky. There were people sitting on couches and lounge chairs, for one thing.

There were people sitting in chairs, along one wall on bar stools with little wooden backs on them. There was a rack of CDs, and everybody was having these strange fuckin' drinks. I didn't know what the fuck they were. They didn't look like fuckin' coffee. They looked more like ice-cream sodas, with mountains of fuckin' whipped cream on top.

I wait in the fuckin' line, we're asshole to belly button like fuckin' cattle waiting to get branded, and I finally get up to the girl.

She says, "You want an el grande? You want a choco lotto carmelo venti macrobioto mocha mocha?"

I says, "Honey, I don't know what kind of fuckin' joint this is. I just want a large coffee and a fresh fuckin' piece of pound cake."

She says, "That's seven dollars." Then she's got the fuckin' balls to have a fuckin' tip cup there. She's gonna charge me seven bucks for a cup of coffee and a piece of fuckin' pound cake and she expects a fuckin' tip.

What the fuck is that? For fuckin' coffee and fuckin' pound cake? They can fuckin' stick it. So I walked out of the fuckin' place and around the fuckin' corner.

I went into a fuckin' Pancake House. The waitress wasn't good lookin' but she was at least friendly. When my fuckin' coffee cup was empty she came over with the fuckin' pot to fill it up.

She says, "You want an el grande? You want a choco lotto carmelo venti macrobioto mocha mocha?"

I got the fuckin' breakfast special. Two eggs over. Homefries, bacon, sausage. A stack of fucking pancakes, and—fuck you, Starbucks—all the coffee you could drink. And they threw in a shot of OJ for free. Pulp. Every once in a while a pit floatin' in there, but otherwise mother fuckin' nature's nectar.

The whole thing came to—you guessed it—seven bucks for the whole ball of wax. I said that's so cheap I'll have a cheese Danish and that was another fuckin' buck. I walked out of the pancake house fuckin' stuffed. I didn't feel like eatin' for the rest of the fuckin' day.

This is the Big Man, the Voice of the People, asking you. What's the fuckin' workin' man supposed to do in a fuckin' world where it costs seven fuckin' bucks for a cup of coffee and a piece of fuckin' pound cake?

What the fuck do they think they are serving over there at fuckin' Starbucks: Liquid fucking gold? Stick it up your fuckin' ass, Starbucks.

26. My Aunt Cee Cee Could Fix This Iraqi War Shit

I'm talking about my ninety-two-year-old Aunt Carmela Calderone, from Bensonhurst, Brooklyn. We call her Aunt Cee Cee. Pound for fuckin' pound (all eighty-six of them), she's thetoughest broad I know, like fuckin' nails.

For years Aunt Cee Cee packed a rod when she left the apartment. One time a guy tried to mug her and she

There's my Aunt Cee Cee, far right in the black dress in front of Pete's Diner on Myrtle Avenue, somewhere around 1945. She's commiserating with Mrs. Candoli, whose nephew Bobby ate her victory garden. (Photo courtesy Brian Merlis, www.brooklynpix.com)

shot him through his foot, taking off a toe. That hindered his ability to flee.

She's ninety-two years old and she still walks to the grocery store and to the vegetable market and still makes her own Sunday gravy and veal parmesan and goes to Mass every morning.

She ain't large—Aunt Cee Cee stands maybe five feet tall. I mean, a fuckin' good-size Labrador retriever could probably eat her in a couple of bites. But don't let her size fool you—when I say Aunt Cee Cee is a hard-ass, you can take it to the fuckin' bank, cause Brooklyn is the hard-ass capital of the world.

I take an oath on my mother, I seen Aunt Cee Cee once chase Fat Vinnie Favara, who collected juice money for Benny the Shylock, down Eighty-third Street with a fuckin' baseball bat, after he threatened to break her son Eddie's legs.

You never saw that piece of shit Fat Vinnie run so fast since the day in 1966 when White Castle was giving away free fuckin' cheeseburgers.

So it occurred to me—we oughta send Aunt Cee Cee over to that fuckin' Iraq. She'd bring some law and order to that fuckin' sandbox. First thing she'll do is smoke

> *She'll hunt down those fuckin' terrorists and stuff 'em so full of lasagna they'll be too fat to strap on those suicide belts.*

out that fuckin' Osama bin Laden. Aunt Cee Cee'll crack his fuckin' towel-wearing skull in half with that wooden spoon she uses to cook with, fuckin' thing's the size of a Louisville Slugger.

That cocksucking bin Laden will never know what the fuck hit him, the piece of shit. Then she'll stick the business end of that spoon up that ratfucker's ass and stir up his guts like a pot of fuckin' puttanesca sauce.

Then she'll carpet-bomb the whole fuckin' country with pork chops from Marzulli's butcher store over there on Thirteenth Avenue. You watch them fuckin' Muslims tear

ass the hell out of there when Aunt Cee Cee starts fling-
ing Marzulli's fat sausages at them.

Then what she'll do is hunt down those fuckin' terrorists and tie them down in chairs and stuff 'em so full
of lasagna they'll be too fuckin' fat to strap on those
suicide belts.

Then she'll show those cocksuckers a picture of Rosie
O'Donnell and say, "Here's what your seventy-two virgins
will look like, you *stronzos*! Go blow yourselves up now."

Then she'll show those goat-humpers a picture of Jersey City and say, "And this is what paradise looks like!"

I'm telling you, Aunt Cee Cee could end that fuckin'
Iraq war in two hours. The goddamn insurgents would
have their hands in the air, waving white flags and shit,
saying, "Please, no more of that little Italian woman!"

27. Taco Bell

About a year ago, people were getting poisoned over at
that Taco Bell. The fuckin' Board of Health shut them
down 'cause everyone's getting that E. coli bacteria. Can't
say I was too surprised when I heard. It wasn't exactly
stunning news. It's not like the fucking Taco Bell has a
reputation for being the most *sanitary* restaurant in the
fucking world.

Most restaurants have a sign in the john that says,
"All employees must wash hands after using restroom."
At Taco Bell, they have a sign that says, "All employees
must piss on their hands after taking a leak."

The Big Man ate at one of them Taco Bell joints one time and let me tell ya, I didn't need no E. coli to make me sick. I ate one of them fuckin' burritos and ten minutes later, badda-bing, ka-boom, ka-boom, I was farting up a storm.

I happened to be in the fuckin' car at the time accompanied by the ol' ball and chain. I started farting so bad my poor wife, Mona, made me stick my ass out the fuckin' window.

> **Women call it "purging."**
> **Men call it stinking up the**
> **fucking place.**

When we got home I barely made it upstairs in time. I was stuck on the fuckin' toilet long enough to read *Gone With the Fuckin' Wind*—which was how Mona felt about then.

I shit enough bricks to rebuild the fuckin' Twin Towers and stunk up the joint so bad, even the fuckin' sewer rats were holding their noses. Peeled the paint right off the fuckin' wall. I think I crapped out a lunch I ate in 1976.

Women call it "purging." Men call it stinking up the fucking place. How do those Mexicans eat that shit? I ate some of them refried beans. Talk about getting a second wind. Now I know how all them illegal aliens get into America. Fuck, one round of that Mexican food and they can blast their asses over the border into fuckin' Texas.

Back in Canarsie if you wanted a good hamburger, you went over to Old Man Kaplan's luncheonette on Rockaway Parkway. Hot off the griddle fresh. From the cow's ass to your plate.

Those were the fuckin' days.

28. Wake Up, England!

So the Big Man was reading where them Islamic schools in England are teaching these young kids that Jews and Christians and pigs and infidels should be slaughtered—five-year-old Muslims kids are being taught to hate! I tell ya, the world's coming to a fuckin' end. And guess who's bankrolling these Muslim schools—that cocksuckin' Saudi royal family.

Then there was a plot they busted up last week over there in London—some Muslim shitbirds kidnap a soldier and cut his fuckin' head off and broadcast it on the Internet.

What the fuck is going on, England? Come on—you Brits used to have balls like coconuts and now those fuckin' Muslims are running your country and you're folding up like cheap suits. And when anyone dares to say a fuckin' word about it, the Muslims attack him and call him a racist. Hey, what kind of shit is that?

Hey Gordon Brown—fuck this global-warming horseshit and grow a pair, would you? Start kickin' those Muslim pricks out of England before you're all prayin' to fuckin' Mecca six times a day.

And America ain't too far behind you Brits, I'm fuckin' sorry to say. It's all 'cause of them fuckin' Saudis, the two-faced cocksuckers. They pretend to be our allies; the fuckers shake with one hand and stab us in the back with the other.

The Big Man says FUCK IRAQ—it's fuckin' Saudi Arabia we oughta be blowing the shit out of. We oughta line them fuckin' Saudi royals up against a wall and pop bullets dipped in pig blood into their fuckin' skulls.

Then the Big Man says, arrest all American son-of-a-whore politicians who've taken a dime of Saudi money and cap their fuckin' greedy asses, too, like that fuckin' peanut farmer Jimmy Carter.

If the Big Man were president, I'd tell those Saudi fucks we're keeping every fuckin' penny they got invested in America. You think you own the Plaza Hotel, Abdullah? Fuck you, we're takin' it back. You got billions of dollars in our banks? Fuck you, we're keeping that, too. Maybe if you stop bankrolling this wahabi shit all over the world, we'll think about givin' it back. You don't, we keep it and then we're gonna nuke your flea-bitten asses. And, hey, stop coming over here to New York and spreadin' bedbugs all over the fuckin' place.

Anyway, think about it.

29. This Is No Stretch: The Kid from Brooklyn Is Born

The Big Man is going to tell you his life story, starting from the very beginning, so get comfortable. This could take a few hours. Mona, get me a drink! I'm going to be talking. What do I want? A fuckin' diet cherry, what the fuck do I usually want?

Where should I start? How about the fuckin' beginning. Whoa, that's a long fuckin' time ago. The world was a different place back then. Kids these days think the world back then was in fuckin' black and white.

That's about as wrong as you can get. There were colors in the olden days. In fact, they were brighter and more vivid than they are today. Today, everything is a little gray from soot and faded with age. When I was young, everything was bright and colorful. It was fuckin' sunny all summer and there was always a nice blanket of white snow in the winter.

April 6, 1947! I was born in Beth-El Hospital now Brookdale Medical Center, along the Brownsville/East New York border. Those are two fuckin' neighborhoods north of the neighborhood I grew up in, the one and only Canarsie: 756 Rockaway Avenue.

The Big Man was *not* an outrageously huge baby. You'd think, but no. Seven eleven. Seven pounds, eleven ounces. Not that the nurses didn't stare at me in wild wonder, but that was a different thing.

But I got big quick, and once I started getting big I didn't stop until I reached my current glorious six five and four-hundred-plus pounds. It's the truth.

When I was a teenager, I lived at 21 Conklin Avenue, between Remsen Avenue and Durland Place. Right next door was the American Legion Post 573.

I lived in Canarsie for as long as I can remember. I was there as an infant, there as a kid, there as a teenager. My fuckin' formative days were in Canarsie. It was a pleasant, blue-collar section of Brooklyn.

Canarsie, in case you lost your fuckin' map, is in easternmost Brooklyn, right up against Jamaica Bay. That's where the Canarsie Piers is. You can see it from the Belt Parkway.

By the time I was born, Canarsie was already more than three fuckin' hundred years old. I looked it up on the Information Super fuckin' Highway. Canarsie's got 312 square blocks. The neighborhood is bordered by Jamaica Bay on the south; Paerdegat Basin and Ralph Avenue on the west; Ditmas Avenue, Avenue D, and Linden Boulevard on the north; and Louisiana Avenue to Fresh Creek Basin on the east.

Canarsie was not the inner city. It was on the water. My house was maybe a mile from the water, tops. Canarsie Beach Park and Canarsie Pier are on Jamaica Bay. They called it the Canarsie Shore.

They say Brooklyn is a fucking polyglot, a melting pot, and that's just what Canarsie was back in the early 1950s. We had every fuckin' nationality. It was like the fuckin' UN. German. Italian, Puerto Rican. Everybody living together, no problem.

When I was a kid I could walk down the street to the candy store and get a Coke. Not out of the bottle or out of the can, like today. They'd make it with the real

Coke syrup and seltzer. I guess there are still soda fountains where you can get the syrup and water mixed right in front of you, but they never get it right. At some fuckin' places you get so much fuckin' syrup that you feel like you're gonna get the fuckin' diabetes before you're finished, and at others it's nothing but stained soda water. Back when I was a kid, they always got the ratio of syrup to water just right and, I wanna tell you, it was the best fuckin' Coke in the fuckin' world, a hundred times better than in a bottle.

You could get a big fat pretzel back in those days. Handmade. Cost a nickel. Today, all you can get are fuckin' machine-made pretzels and they want three bucks for 'em. Back in those days, everything was pure.

I remember going to the pizzeria and you could get a whole fuckin' pizza for a dollar, and I could eat a whole pizza, so I know. And it was better than what you pay twenty dollars for today. The dough, the sauce, and everything else was made from scratch.

Today, the pizza is made of fuckin' cardboard. The fuckin' world is coming to an end.

The main drag in Canarsie is Rockaway Parkway. In those days, there was only one movie theater in the neighborhood. That was the Canarsie at South Third Street and Avenue L. For half a buck, you got a double feature and a cartoon. I remember going to see *The Vikings*— Kirk Douglas, Tony Curtis, Ernest Borgnine. Great fuckin' picture. Lots of blondes, too, with big *cazongas*.

30. A Little More About the Kid

I went to Public School 114. My principal was Mr. Bricker. He was like a god. The thought of getting sent to Mr. Bricker's office, shot—you'd fuckin' rather deal with Saint Peter at the fuckin' pearly gates.

I never had to go see Mr. Bricker too much, though. I was mostly a good kid, except for the time I farted during an air-raid drill.

I went to Junior High School 211, also in Canarsie, and Samuel J. Tillman High School, which was in the East Flatbush section of Brooklyn. Then I transferred to Food Trades High School, which was on West Thirteenth Street and Eighth Avenue in Manhattan.

I had a lot of friends and they all had nicknames. Like this kid Tommy Malone. We called him Shorty. That was because he was short. Me, they always called Big Mike, ever since I can remember, because I was big.

This kid Richard Leone, they called him "Butler." He looked like one of them butlers in a British movie.

We had Hairy Tony. Fourteen years old and he had hair on his back.

Frankie Shorts. He'd go into a store and shortchange the guy all the time.

Danny Fingers. They called him Danny Fingers because he had extralong fingers. Like you could imagine them having an extra knuckle they were so fuckin' long.

Pete the Killer. They didn't call him Pete the Killer because he was a killer. They called him Pete the Killer because you never saw him wearing the same clothes twice. He dressed emaculately and the girls loved him.

I had a friend named Benjy Everything. He just died, in fact. He was a jack of all fuckin' trades. His willingness to please was never-ending, as long as the price was fuckin' right. And his ability to please was extraordinary, taking into consideration the fuckin' oddball requests he got. Bottom line: If you needed something, Benjy'd get it for you. He didn't care if you needed a broad, a stove, an air conditioner, or a bottle of liquor. He'd get you a pair of pants, socks, whatever the fuck you needed. Benjy Everything could get anything. He was like the old-fashioned peddler. He'd get you what you wanted and then you'd pay him off every week, two, three dollars a week.

His was a business with as little overhead as possible. You heard of the fuckin' one-man band? That was Benjy Everything. He was a one-man business. He was even

Tessie Triple Nipple. She managed to keep her third tit a secret until an August heat wave made her sweat right through her blouse. (Photo courtesy Brian Merlis, www.brooklynpix.com)

his own bookkeeper. He'd carry a book with him and when you gave him money, he'd pull out this book and make a note of it. Benjy Everything was what ya call fuckin' organized. A helluva guy. People took him wrong, though. They thought he was cheap.

Then there was Cutter. The kid wasn't called Cutter because he cut anybody. He was a baseball pitcher and he threw a hard-breaking ball, so he was Cutter. The cops found out he was called Cutter and hassled him for a while. They thought he got the name because he was using a knife on people.

Then there were guys who had a couple of reasons for the same nickname. Take Murray the Muff. Murray the Muff wore a wig. He would go down on a woman and his wig would come off when he was doing it, so they called him Murray the Muff.

There was Tessie Triple Nipple. She had three tits. Nobody knew why.

Some nicknames were just shouted out one day and they kind of stuck. Others were fuckin' hard earned. Take, for example, Richie Dickhead. You'd think that since his fuckin' first name was Richard that he'd be known as Dickie Dickhead or something like that, but no. The dickhead had nothing to do with his first name. It had to do with the fuckin' head of his dick. You know that movie *A Christmas Story* where the fuckin' stupid kid gets double-dog dared into sticking his tongue on the fuckin' flagpole and it gets frozen there? Well, Richie was taking a leak by the flagpole one really cold Brooklyn mornin' and we double-fuckin' dog dared him to stick his dick on the flagpole, which he did.

The firemen didn't come, like in the fuckin' movie.

Just the school nurse with rubbing alcohol. And that was how he got to be Richie Dickhead. He claims that the resulting scar tissue has given him an advantage in later years, but I don't know about that. For weeks there was a rumor that Richie's dickhead was still stuck to the flag-pole but I never mustered up the fuckin' nads to look. Who the fuck wants to see that?

That's the way Brooklyn was in those days.

31. Having Fun

I grew up without a father. He died when I was four. My mom did the best she could and we got by. And I had a lot of fun. I had friends and we didn't need much to have fun. Anything was fun. Everything was fun.

I remember me and my friends getting on the LL train, the Canarsie line. It's called the L line today but it runs on the same track. Back then some of the BMT trains were double letters, GG, RR, LL, etc.

We'd get on and just ride the train. For fun. Not because we were going anywhere. We'd get on at the Rock-away Parkway stop and ride it all the way to Eighth Avenue in Manhattan.

Then we'd ride it back again. It was a subway in Man-hattan but some of the time it was elevated and you could look out the window and watch all of fuckin' Brooklyn go by.

Other times, we'd get on the bus. You got a paper transfer back in those days. We'd get on a bus in Canarsie, get a transfer, and go out to Coney Island. Get a fuckin' foot-long hotdog at Nathan's.

Since we didn't have any money we played games that didn't involve a lot of equipment. Not like today when a parent has to shell out hundreds of dollars so the kid can play lacrosse or some fuckin' Ivy League sport.

We'd play handball, stoopball, stickball. You could buy a rubber ball for a nickel and play eighty different games with it, and it never broke. If you were careful, one ball could last you the whole fuckin' summer.

The ball was pink and hollow and called a Spaldeen, even though the word didn't appear on it. All it said was "Spalding," which was the name of the sporting goods company that made them. The company was founded by Al Spalding who was a star pitcher in nineteenth-century baseball—back in the days when they had handlebar fuckin' mustaches and drank big steins of Pabst Blue Ribbon right on the field.

If we didn't have a fuckin' Spaldeen, we'd use a Pennsy Pinkie, which was short for Pennsylvania Pinkie. It was the same size as a Spaldeen, maybe a millimeter bigger, but it was solid rubber and cost a fuckin' dime. Either way, the fuckin' ball lasted until it went over a fence or got stuck on a roof.

We used to make our own scooters. You know those little folding Razor scooters them kids scoot around on today? Well, ours were handmade. We'd start with a pair of roller skates and a two by four. Then we'd take a good old-fashioned wooden soda crate, and we'd decorate the whole thing with the soda caps. The trick was not to get clipped by a bus.

We'd flip baseball cards. You know the game? It's like

pitching pennies. You flip the cards toward a wall or a line on the ground, and whoever's closest gets everyone's cards.

I wish I had the cards that I flipped now. Some of those cards would be worth hundreds of dollars today. I'm talking a 1956 Mickey Mantle card—that was the Mick's MVP year— and I'm flipping it into the dirt along Conklin Avenue. Who fuckin' knew? Mantle wasn't Duke Snider, that's all the fuck I knew.

Sometimes I used to go hang out at a place called the Brownsville Boys Club, on Linden Boulevard. It cost a dollar for a whole year and you could go swimming in the pool there. Right across the street from the Brownsville Boys' Club you had Coney Island Joe's. He used to make the hotdogs. He didn't use the regular frankfurter roll. He'd give it to you on French bread. Onions, sauerkraut. You got terrible gas but it was well worth it. I can still taste those onions. I burp just thinking about them.

Ebbets Field, where the Brooklyn Dodgers used to play before those son of a bitch bastards moved to fuckin' Los Angeles. (Photo courtesy Brian Merlis, www.brooklynpix.com)

32. The Brooklyn Dodgers

Ebbets Field. Now there was a fucking ballpark. Not like today. It had character. The outfield walls were all uneven so you never knew how the ball was going to bounce when it hit them. Only Carl Furillo knew. He always knew.

It's no news to you twenty-first-century readers that the Brooklyn Dodgers story ain't got no happy ending. They broke the fuckin' heart of all of Brooklyn, in the long run.

It was sad. The Dodgers left town when I was ten, eleven years old, but I was lucky enough to see them Boys of Summer play in Brooklyn, fifteen, twenty times before they split for the West Coast.

The ballpark was on the east side of Prospect Park. There's a fucking housing development there now and a fucking sign that says, "No Ballplaying." There's a nice mural today across the street from where the ballpark used to be, of all the Dodgers from the 1955 World Championship team, Jackie Robinson in the middle.

It hurt Brooklyn bad when the Dodgers left. It was like they tore the fucking heart right out of the whole fucking city. You know, borough. City. It's nice that they've got minor-league baseball at Coney Island now. That's better than nothing, but it ain't the same.

My mother didn't have the time or the money to be taking me to no ballgames, but every once in a while someone would treat me to a game. It only cost a half buck to get in, back then, and we'd sit up on the roof.

You probably heard about the "Cowbell Lady" they had out there in centerfield. Well, I swear to my mother, she was the ugliest woman in Brooklyn. She was working a full-growth beard.

The fuckin' neighborhood around the ballpark wasn't as good as it used to be and they crammed as many asses into that place as they could. Fuck, those seats were fuckin' small. Ebbets Field smelled like rust and cigars. It was a good smell.

I wouldn't eat in the ballpark. Every time I went to see the Dodgers play, my mother would give me a dollar to eat. After the game I'd take that dollar and go to the White Castle. For a buck you could get ten hamburgers and a soda.

I had no animosity growing up. I had no gripes. I had more fun with a dollar back then than people can have today for a thousand.

33. Growing Up Quick

When I was a teenager I grew up quick. I wasn't with kids my own age no more. I had outgrown them, in a couple of ways. I was more fuckin' mature than the other kids my age—and I was much bigger. When I was fourteen I looked like I was twenty-five, and I was already almost as wide as I am now, so a lot of people took me for being older.

I just couldn't be with the kids my own age no more. I started hanging with grown men. Guys forty, fifty, sixty years old. They were generous to me and it was just because they liked me. They didn't want no favors in return or nothing.

These guys gave me a taste of the good life—and once that happens, you can never go back. By the time I was fifteen and in high school, I was into booze, broads, and fucking horseflesh.

They were great guys and they fuckin' took great care of me. You wanna know who they were? The names. I'll tell you. I remember it like it was yesterday. There was Tony Santo, Abie the Jew, Joe Peanuts, Danny Fingers, Bobby Brooks, and Joe the Plumber. Great guys.

They took me under their wing and showed me the ropes. They treated me like one of their own, these men. Maybe some of them didn't know I was as young as I was. Like I said, I looked older.

They took me to the racetrack every night. Sometimes they took me to whorehouses. Or McTweedies Bar and Grill.

There was a time there in my fuckin' youth when the Big Man was quite the aficionado in the fuckin' world of professional women. They really did have red lights in the window.

Most of the whorehouses were up in Harlem. They had women of all colors there. The Big Man didn't care about color. I'll never forget I went to the doctor once when I was kid. His name was Dr. Diamond. He was on Ninety-third Street and Flatland Avenue. He was an old-time doctor. I was fifteen, sixteen years old.

I said, "Doctor, I been with a couple of them colored women. You don't think I'm going to get a disease, do ya?"

He said, "Big Mike, as long as they're clean, makes no difference. The color don't rub off."

The crew over at McTweedie's Bar and Grill in Canarsie.
Left to right: Sneed Hearn, head bartender; Jimmy "One
Eye" Caponata, who's eating what looks like a live duck;
Grady Flick, dishwasher and part-time bouncer; Francis
Xavier McTweedie, who owned the joint; Happy Perkins,
the griddle man who thought grease was a major food
group; and Lazlo "the Mad Hungarian" Shmecki, who
mopped the floor and got to clean the men's room—
good experience for when he moved back to Hungary
and became the mayor of Budapest. (Photo courtesy
Brian Merlis, www.brooklynpix.com)

Most of the time we went up to Harlem, but they had
whorehouses in Crown Heights in them days, too. We
went there. You know, you pick the girl you want and
you go and nobody watches you and you do what you
got to do in private.

After we all got our fuckin' rocks off, we'd go out for
a big meal. The guys liked to watch me eat. I think that

was the basis for our relationship. They gave me whores and a taste of the Sport of Kings, and I put on a show when we got to the dinner table.

I could eat and eat and eat, I'm a big fuckin' man, and these guys thought this was a riot. They loved to fuckin' watch me eat and I always did my best not to disappoint them.

I was fuckin' putting on a show for their entertainment—and they never stopped enjoying it. Since they ate in great restaurants, I got to eat there, too. Steaks, seafood, fuckin' Italian food.

Sometimes these fuckin' guys would take me to the pool hall. We usually shot eight ball but every once in a while we'd shoot straight pool; you had to remember to call your shot. Once or twice we shot nine ball because they showed it on TV, Willie Mosconi and Minnesota Fats, and it was the craze for, like, two days.

In Canarsie, goin' to the fuckin' pool hall meant Pop Klee's place. There were only six tables in the joint. The place was on East Ninety-fourth Street, between Avenues L and M.

Pop Klee, he also sold fishin' bait and tackle. You know, poles and lures and live bait and shit. So it was a bait store/pool hall. Only in fuckin' Canarsie. Perfect combo of dark saloon and bayside breeze.

You had gang members in the late fifties who went fishin'. Juvenile delinquents with the curl of Vitalis hair on their forehead and skintight dungarees heading down to the Canarsie shore with a pole, bucket, and tackle box.

We shot pool in Pop Klee's. I wasn't a fisherman so I never bought any bait or tackle. Pop Klee charged fifty cents an hour to play on one of his tables. Good tables, too. The big ones, not the little coin-operated eight-ball tables you find sometimes in your whatcha-call bar and grill.

I learned how to play poker. I got jobs dealing at poker games; guys didn't want to deal their own cards. Every time someone would win a pot, they'd throw the dealer a couple of bucks. When I had a hundred bucks saved up, they'd let me play for a while, and sometimes they'd win their tip money right back.

And all of that was while I was still in fucking high school. No wonder I developed a fuckin' gambling problem!

34. Me and John Gotti Have a Coffee

When I tell people that the Big Man knew John Gotti, they tell me I'm full of shit. But the Big Man is here to tell you it's no shit at all. Me and Johnny Boy—that's what we called John Gotti back then—we grew up half a fuckin' mile from each other in Brooklyn. He had his crew, guys like Tony "Roach" Rampino and Sal Ruggerio and Johnny's older brother Peter, along with Frankie DeCicco and Jimmy Brown Faillia from over in Marine Park. Those fucks would shoot you in the kneecaps and laugh their crazy asses off when you howled in pain. Then they'd go out to Chopper Malarkey's Bowl-a-Rama on Avenue W and snort down a couple of pitchers of beer and make fun of the fat housewives who were lucky if they could knock down one pin on the first toss.

John Gotti needs no introduction. If you follow this stuff, then you know Johnny Boy had the head of the whole fuckin' Gambino family, Big Paul Castellano, whacked in front of Sparks Steak House in Manhattan back in December 1985. Johnny ran the Gambino outfit for fifteen years before the fucking feds ran him down and tossed him into that maximum-security shithole in Illinois. The fucking State of Illinois let him rot with cancer and didn't do shit to help him. But that's another story.

The Big Man's here to tell you he knew John Gotti pretty good and, yeah, he was far from fuckin' perfect, he had some blood on his hands. But to our way of thinking in Brooklyn, he was just a businessman, no better or no worse than those chiselers on Wall Street or those Enron greedheads. The only difference was, Johnny Boy cut a few corners on his way up the ladder to success. Yeah, he littered the streets of Brooklyn and Queens with fuckin' bodies. And whatever you've read about him in the newspapers about his being a ruthless killer, all I can say is, when you're the boss of an outfit like the Gambinos, you got to be ready to do some unpleasant shit.

Johnny used to hang out with his crew at the Ravenite Social Club on Mulberry Street in Little Italy. That is, when he wasn't hanging his coat at the Bergin Hunt and Fish Club out there in Howard Beach, Queens, where he ran his crew. As far as the Big Man knows, Johnny's widow, Victoria, still lives there.

The Ravenite was on the ground floor of an old tenement building, right between Mickey d'Arco's Casa

Italiana (Mickey made a kick-ass osso buco) and Vito Moscarella's Liquor Store.

So one day the Big Man gets a call from Tinky Vitale. Tinky says, "Hey, Big Man, I need three front row center for the Sunday matinee of that fuckin' *Cats.* For my fucking mother-in-law and a couple of her golden-girl pals. You fix it up, okay?"

Well, it was already Saturday afternoon and that was cutting it pretty fucking close, but it Tinky Vitale. He was one of Johnny's oldest pals, ran a bunch of his rackets out in Flatlands and Marine Park, loansharking and gambling and shit. He said, "I'll be with the big guy downtown at the place when Vito brings the stuff. But if you see me smoking a Camel, keep walking."

In Tinky talk, that meant meet him Sunday morning at the Ravenite, the "big guy downtown" being Gotti, with the tickets, around noon—Vito Moscarella always brought a big box of cannolis and bottles of Scotch and anisette and grappa, that kick-ass Sicilian moonshine, to the Ravenite—Vito's weekly gift to the Godfather. I already knew about the Camels. Tinky's cigarette of choice was Parliaments. He only smoked Camels when he was being tailed by the fucking feds.

So I hauled my ass down to the Ravenite on Sunday morning. Gotti was already there, in one of them $2,000 custom-made silk suits he loved so much, not a fucking one of his silver hairs out of place. He was sitting at a card table, screaming at his brother Peter and that rat prick Sammy "the Bull" Gravano.

Now, the Big Man knew John Gotti from the old neighborhood when he ran with a gang of real hard-asses called the Rockaway Boys. Pound for pound, the Rockaways were the toughest gang in Brooklyn and Queens. Hijacking trucks out at Kennedy, stolen car rings, armed robbery, the whole fuckin' ball of wax. Nobody fucked with the Rockaways.

Truth was, I was hoping to get to the Ravenite before Johnny showed up—one twitch of his left eyebrow and you ended up the bottom of fuckin' Sheepshead Bay with a slot machine tied around your gullet. I mean, he was okay to the Big Man—we never had any beefs or nothing. Shit, if we did, you wouldn't be reading this now. I was welcome at the Ravenite 'cause I got all the guys tickets for half price and I didn't ask questions.

Johnny was screaming pretty good, spraying saliva in Peter and the Bull's faces. "I don't give a fuck if his fuckin' hemorrhoids are bleedin', you tell Joey Fish to get his ass over to the joint in Ozone Park by noon or I'm gonna staple his fuckin' balls to the top of the fuckin' Chrysler Building. You hear me? I'll burn his fuckin' house down, I'll ass-fuck his ninety-year-old mother!" Joey Coluccio had a fish market over on Fort Hamilton Parkway out in Borough Park. Like everyone else in John Gotti's world, he was a degenerate gambler. He always smelled like flounder and owed every bookie in Brooklyn. Joey Fish had been ducking Gotti and his crew for weeks.

Peter G. yelled back at his brother (and Peter was the *only* one who could yell back at Johnny), "I'm tellin' you, the Fish is fuckin' MIA. I got Tony Zits and Patty Cusimano looking in every rathole from Coney Island to the fuckin' Bronx for the guy. Word is, he's layin' low in Lauderdale."

Johnny's face was turning the color of a blood blister.

He growled, "He's been back for a fuckin' week, you jerkoffs. At his mother's place in fuckin' Ridgewood."

I figured maybe it was a good time to step outside until the Gotti shitstorm blew over. I turned to leave and Johnny Boy looked at me quick and said, "Don't go nowhere."

Not missing a beat, his shitfit continued. "You tell that fucking *stronzo* Fish he better have my ninety grand or I'm gonna put his wife to work turnin' fuckin' tricks on Tenth Avenue," Gotti went on. "You tell that piece of shit I'll bury his kids alive in a fuckin' landfill and make him watch, *capisce*?"

Peter G and that rat cocksucker Sammy the Bull left to track down Joey Fish. It wasn't the ninety grand—Johnny dropped that much and more in one afternoon of football. It was about respect. John Gotti was the boss and nobody owed him. It was also about the ninety grand.

Gotti turned to me and gave me a huge grin, his anger gone. He said, "Big Mike, how the fuck you doin'?"

"I'm doin' good, John," I said. "I got Tinky V's tickets."

Johnny said, "You believe he's gonna pay to see that shit? I swear to Christ, Tinky's turnin' into a fuckin' homo." I didn't mention to Gotti that the tickets were for Tinky's mother-in-law. Let Tinky sweat that one later.

"That fat fuck Tinky ain't here," Johnny said. "He had to go uptown to check on that shit for Frankie D." I had no fuckin' idea what he's talking about and I don't fuckin' ask. Gotti says, "Sit down, for Chrissake, have a fuckin' coffee." (Coffee meant espresso.)

The Big Man sat.

He tells Tony Roach to get me a coffee. Tony "Roach"

Rampino was one of Johnny's oldest and most loyal gorillas, from back in their Rockaway days. Tony Roach liked the needle. He was tall and skinnier than a screen door, had those sunken cheeks and tiny black eyes, a cross between Peter Lorre and fuckin' Charlie Manson. Johnny hated fuckin' junkies (even if his crew was hustling a lot of the shit and making a fuckin' fortune) but he put up with Tony Roach, who'd been a pretty handy part of the hit team that took down Big Paul Castellano and his asshole driver and bodyguard Tommy Bilotti in front of Spark's Steakhouse in 1985.

While the Roach is wrestling with the antique espresso maker, Johnny picks up a deck of cards and starts futzin' around with them, layin' down a game of solitaire. Then he says, "So things are good, Big Mike? You making a living?"

"Yeah," I tell him, "I'm gettin' by." Johnny nods and takes a sip of his espresso. He barks at Tony Roach, "Where's them cannolis Sally brung? You wanna cannoli, Big Mike?"

What I fuckin' wanted was my three bills from Tinky Vitale for those fuckin' *Cats* tickets so I could be on my fuckin' way. Instead, Tony Roach throws a cannoli on a paper plate and slaps it down on the table. Roach squirts out a couple of espressos and sets them down. Gotti starts stirring his, taking his sweet fuckin' time.

"That fuckin' Fish," he says. "I gotta do something about that bastard." Coffee, a cannoli, and conversation with John Gotti—nothing good was coming out of this. Any hopes I had of making a quick exit from the Ravenite were in the toilet. When John Gotti gave you a cannoli, you ate.

"You know that piece of shit Joey Fish, don't you?" Johnny asks me.

I knew Joey Fish to maybe say hello and that's it. I say,"A little bit, not too much."

"The fucking cheap cocksucker is in to me for ninety large," Gotti says.

"Man's gotta hustle a lot of scungilli for ninety large," I say. I'd already heard Johnny's opinion of Joey Fish.

"And he sells shit fish," Gotti goes on. "Went in to his joint last year to buy some clams, he don't shut up about how great this sea bass he has, just came in from Chile or one of them shithole greaser countries down there. I tell him, 'I ain't eatin' no spic fish. Ain't you got any Chile sea bass that's local?' I mean, what the fuck, right?"

Maybe if I eat the cannoli quick, I can get the hell out of there. So I finish it off in two big bites, wash it down with that fuckin' axle grease Tony Roach called espresso.

"Good shit, those cannolis," Gotti says. "From Ferrara's. Hey, Roach, get the Big Man another one."

Tony Roach gave me another cannoli. Gotti says to him, "Give the Big Man more coffee, too."

I say—and it's outta my big yap before I can stop myself—"That's okay, Johnny. I gotta head out to see Boozy d'Amico—"

Johnny cuts me off with a glare cold enough to freeze 200-proof grappa. I get the message. Boozy's gonna wait.

Gotti keeps stirring his espresso. Five more minutes and he'll be churning butter. He says, "You know, Big Man, I'm tired. You wanna fuckin' know why? 'Cause I got nothing but fuckin' jerkoffs and shitheads working for me. Dopers, crackheads, fuckin' piss drunks." He shakes his head, looking sad. "I'm telling you, this thing of ours is in the fucking toilet. I can't find nobody I can hardly trust—every shitbird in town's tryin' to pork me up the butt. Like this fuckin' *gavone* Joey Fish."

Now, I like Johnny for the most part, but this conversation's going in a direction that ain't exactly to my liking. Plus my big ass is getting pretty goddamn squirmy in that crappy folding chair. It was good for maybe one cheek so I had to keep switching from one to the other. Shit, the tons of dough these wiseguys pulled in, you think they'd spring for some comfortable fuckin' furniture. It ain't common knowledge, but a lot of wiseguys were some of the stingiest cocksuckers on the fuckin' planet. I remember one from back in Canarsie, Eddie "Spoons" Manganaro—he got his nickname for stealing the spoons from Midnight Sadie's luncheonette on Livonia Avenue 'cause he was too fuckin' cheap to buy his own silverware.

"Yeah," I agree, trying to play it safe. "They don't build 'em like they fuckin' used to. Remember when Tommy Funzi torched the wrong pizzeria on Woodhaven Boulevard? He was pissed at Carmine LoPresti but he put the match to Allie Boy Grimaldi's joint—"

Gotti wasn't much for small talk. He leans toward me and lowers his voice. "How'd youse like to help me out on something, Big Mike?"

There was no wiggling out of this one. I say, "Well, sure, I guess so, Johnny."

"How'd you like to put the blast on Joey Fish?" Gotti asks.

I *knew* that's where Gotti was going with this. It all made sense now. He didn't want any of his boys clipping Joey Fish cause Joey was with the Bonannos and Gotti was Gambino. What Gotti was supposed to do in a case like this is have a sit-down with the Bonannos and get permission to whack Joey. But Gotti's attitude was, "I don't fuckin' answer to nobody. If I wanna whack the Fish, I'm gonna whack his ass." By having an outsider do the job—that outsider being me—the Bonannos couldn't make a beef on Gotti and start a whole shitstorm.

The Big Man grew up around a lotta wiseguys and was friendly with some of them. But I never went into the "life," as they say. You got to be able to kill people to have any success in the life, and I couldn't kill nobody. And you got to have a taste for violence, something else I didn't have. Shit, I can't stand the sight of blood. Especially when it's my own. Which I guess is why Gotti saw me as the perfect candidate to do the job. I'm the last guy anyone would suspect.

Something else to keep in mind: Dead men tell no tales. Even if I did have the balls to fuckin' kill Joey Fish, Gotti would have me killed a week later so the murder couldn't be traced back to him. He'd have his boys put two bullets behind my left ear and either bury me somewhere in the fuckin' country or take me out to an auto junkyard on Pennsylvania Avenue and chop me up into a dozen bloody chunks. That's how these guys operate. I mean, shit, I've always wanted to be a man about town but preferably in one piece.

So here were my options, and they sucked: (1) I could

tell Gotti flat out I wouldn't do it, in which case he might kill me anyway, or (2) I could do the job on Joey Fish and, for sure, I'd be whacked. I decided to go with the first option.

I said, "Johnny, you know I ain't ever whacked nobody and I'd probably just fuck it up. Plus everybody knows me. Was I you, I'd bring in some talent from Boston or maybe Pittsburgh."

I could see Gotti thinking it over. God was looking out for me that day 'cause right then Tinky Vitale walked into the place and wanted his tickets and I was off the hook. Tinky tried to chisel me down on the price and this time I let him 'cause I just wanted to get the fuck out of there.

I don't know if Joey Fish ever got whacked or not. I didn't ask and no one was talking, which suited me fine. I steered clear of the Ravenite Social Club and John Gotti after that 'cause, if it wasn't Joey Fish, there was always somebody else he wanted dead. My mother had a saying: Lie down with dogs, wake up with fleas. I ain't saying Gotti was a dog—I liked him, as I said—but a lotta guys got themselves killed by Johnny and his crew, sometimes for stupid things like not returning his phone call right away.

The Big Man is happy to report he wasn't one of them.

35. Tommy the Twitch

That reminds me of another scalpin' story. There was one guy worked outside all the ballparks named Tommy the Twitch. He was kind of a nervous fella with a high-pitched voice. He talked fast. It sounded like they'd recorded his voice and were playin' it back at the wrong speed.

This fuckin' story takes place like more than forty fuckin' years ago. This was back in the days when the New York Mets were brand spankin' new. The Dodgers split for L.A. The Giants went to Frisco. Here came the Mets. Everyone was psyched. Of course those Mets were some of the worst teams ever but for fans it didn't fuckin' matter. When the Mets first came around, they were a hot ticket.

The Mets played their first couple years at the Polo Grounds, where fuckin' Firpo knocked Dempsey out of the ring. After a couple of years up on 155th Street, the Mets built their own stadium out near where they were having the World's Fair at the time, out in Willets Point. The Mets sucked big time but nobody cared. They drank another beer. Everybody had fuckin' Mets fever. And us scalpers, we weren't always exactly honest.

But all scalpers did it. Truth was, no matter where the ticket was, even if it was in the nosebleed seats with a better view of downtown Flushing than of the Shea infield, we would say that the tickets were "right behind the Mets dugout."

Every single ticket being sold by every single scalper at every single Shea game was "right behind the Mets dugout." The rule of thumb was nobody ever called you on the deception.

They were glad that they'd gotten into the game, and many were hip enough to bribe a fuckin' usher, in which case they might actually get to sit behind the fuckin' Mets dugout. And, of course, the scalpers were long gone, scattered to the fuckin' winds, by the time the crowd let out.

Which brings me back to this little guy named Tommy the Twitch. He was about five four. He was a good little hustler. We called him the Twitch on account of every once in a while half his face would lurch. You'd

"Who needs tickets? Who needs tickets here? Right behind the Mets dugout!" Tommy the Twitch would bark.

think he was winkin' at you about something, then you'd realize he couldn't fuckin' help it. Tommy the Twitch used the Mets dugout in his chant.

"Who needs tickets? Who needs tickets here? Right behind the Mets dugout!" Tommy the Twitch would bark.

So this guy—a big guy, about six two, two fifty—came up to Tommy and he said, "Give me five."

And Tommy sold him seats that were in the upper deck, in the outfield, with a view obstructed by the foul pole! They were three-dollar tickets and Tommy charged the guy ten each.

The guy went into the fucking game. Twitchy was running around. About a half-hour later, the big guy came back out of the ballpark and went straight for Twitch. In a flash he had the little guy up against the fucking Shea Stadium wall, with one hand. Twitch's feet were off the ground.

"Give me my money back, you little cocksucker!" the guy said. Twitch was hittin' fuckin' green. He gave the guy his money back. But that was the only time I saw anyone come back out, no matter how far the seats were from really being behind the Mets dugout, or the Yankees dugout, or the Rangers bench, or the Knicks bench.

I miss those days. You used to meet the craziest characters. Today, it's the end of the world.

The plainclothes guys grabbed me many times. They would give you a summons. It was like paying a tax on the fuckin' money you made by fuckin' scalpin' tickets. Sometimes the fine was fifty. Sometimes it was a hundred.

36. The History of My Stomach

If there's one thing the Big Man knows how to do well and often, it's eat. You may wonder where I learned to eat like I do. I guess you'd have to blame my mother for being such a good cook. For the Big Man and food, it was love at first sight.

Now, my mother didn't have a lot of money, so we

weren't having any fancy kinds of meat or anything like that. But everything she made was great. We'd have pasta fazoo spaghetti and meatballs, veal cutlets.

Once I got to be fourteen, fifteen and hanging around with the older guys, that's when I first began to go to restaurants and learning about some of the finer things in life, food-wise. My favorite one was Don Peppe's, or, as they used to call it, Velsilvio's. It was on the corner of Cleveland and Liberty in Brooklyn.

The guy who owned Velsilvio's was called Sal the Sheik. He was a button guy. You know what I mean when I say that? He was a made man. We used to go there. That's where all the jockeys went to eat. Angel Cordero, Bobby Ussery.

Another place they used to take me was Crisci's on Lorimer and Conselyea in the South Side section of Brooklyn. That's right near the East River, between Williamsburg and Greenpoint, south of the Brooklyn/Queens border.

Those were the Italian places. When we wanted steak, we went to Luchow's at 110 East 14th Street, between

You could see everyone in Ratner's. Movie stars. Gangsters. And the food was great. They had a buffet with cheese blintzes, potato latkes, split pea soup.

Third and Fourth avenues in Manhattan. They said it was the most famous German restaurant in the country, and I guess it was. It's a shopping center now, right across from the Zeckendorf Towers, which weren't there when I was a kid, either. The building that housed Luchow's was there until the mid-1990s. Then they had a suspicious fire and the whole block got torn down for new shiny buildings. Luchow's had been there since the 1800s. When it was new, it was in the so-called theater district. This was when vaudeville was all the rage and before the main theaters moved uptown to Broadway in the Times Square area.

If we were in the mood for Jewish, we'd go to Ratner's on Delancey Street. It had been there since 1918. It stayed open until 2002. The number of Jewish immigrants in the Lower East Side kept shrinking and the place couldn't survive on the whatchacall goy trade.

But back in the day, you could see everyone in Ratner's. Movie stars. Gangsters. And the food was great. They had a buffet with cheese blintzes, potato latkes, split pea soup. I always thought Ratner's was best at one, two in the morning. When you sat down, they'd right away give you a whole basket of fresh-made onion rolls.

But my favorite restaurant is Peter Luger's. I've been going there since I was fifteen and I never had a bad steak. Peter Luger's: the best steak in the world.

Sometimes we'd go to the Second Avenue Deli in the East Village. You would get all the pickles, all the peppers you want for nothin'. They're out of business now, but they were one of my favorite places. The owner, Abe, got murdered. He had a bank deposit. They never caught the guy, either.

A lot of things piss me off. Cell phones. Pizza at $2.50 a fuckin' slice. Politicians. Muslim terrorists. Starbucks. The price of gasoline. The world's coming to a fuckin' end. (Photo courtesy Kevin Helmick)

37. Things That Piss Me Off

Back when I was a kid, everything was pure and simple. Now things are polluted and complicated. If you needed something back in my day you went to the right guy, gave him a few dollars, and it would be done.

If you wanted a driver's license, if you wanted to build an extension on your house, you paid the guy and it was done. Today you got to go though the red tape.

If I had to fuckin' list the fuckin' things that make me nuts, greed would be number one. There's too much greed in the United States today. Listen. When a person reaches one hundred million dollars in wealth, I think the government should say, "That's it. You can't make no more. Anything else you make, you gotta pay ninety percent in tax."

Give the money to the fuckin' poor people.

Because who the fuck needs more than one hundred fuckin' million dollars? The average guy gets a hundred million, he's never gonna be able to spend it.

Why you gotta be fuckin' greedy? It's not enough to live in a fuckin' three-million-dollar house. They gotta live in a fuckin' thirty- or forty-million-dollar house.

Some of the houses in the Hamptons go for sixty, seventy million. I mean, what do you need a house like that for? Greed becomes a big factor here.

Speakin' of greed, how 'bout that fuckin' Donald Trump. He's a greedy bastard. I don't want to mention any names but I got my sources, the guy is a lousy tipper. Mr. Fifteen Percent. That's fuckin' Trump.

Here's a guy who was born with a silver spoon up his ass. He's a phony billionaire. Banks own 98 percent of Donald Trump. Trump Tower, Trump golf course, Trump fuckin' this, Trump fuckin' that. All owned by the fuckin' bank.

He's payin' the mortgage every fuckin' month just like a workin' Joe. His casino went bankrupt in Atlantic City. He can't get a gaming license in Las Vegas. What's that tell ya?

The number two thing that pisses me off would be the government. I'm not afraid to say it. A lot of people would be afraid. The fuckin' truth is, the government's corrupt. They cover up for one another.

Today, the U.S. government is doing the same job that, years ago, would have been done by the Mafia. It's fuckin' white-collar crime at an unbelievably huge scale. The government is the new Mafia. There's no question about it. They do whatever the fuck they want, and they don't have to be accountable to anybody.

Anything they want. I want to see what's going to happen with this Halliburton thing and Cheney. He's another greedy bastard. I hope the scales of fuckin' justice get the rat bastard.

I'd like to see the vice president do fuckin' time in jail. I don't know if they can impeach a vice president, but if they can they should. Or just arrest him. Doesn't it strike anyone in the attorney general's office or anyone on the Supreme Court a little funny that Cheney was the fuckin' CEO of Halliburton and they're the ones who got all the contracts when we went to war in fuckin' Iraq?

Whenever there's a war, there's a select few who make a fortune. It's bad for almost everybody but, to a chosen few, it's worth billions of dollars. When those few are also deciding whether we go to war, I feel mighty sorry for the moms and dads whose boys and girls volunteered to go in the service, because they are brave and sincere, and they are being used so that a few corrupt people can make a fuckin' buck.

When Cheney retired from Halliburton they gave him millions of dollars, but they got it back. Oh yeah, they got it back all right. A hundredfold. They got to cater the fucking war.

And how about them Bushes. This George W., he didn't even win the first election. I don't know exactly what went on down there with those fuckin' hangin' chads and all, but it was damned fishy.

I wanna know in what country when the majority of the people voted for you and your name is Al Gore, you get screwed by the electoral vote, and the deciding state is run by the brother of your opponent. In what other country in the world would that fuckin' shit be allowed to go on?

You got it right from me. I'm not as polished as most people but more people voted for Gore than voted for Bush but Bush got to be president anyway. We should have known right then that a bunch of corrupt bastards were taking over.

And nobody investigates these fuckin' things. Why, I don't know.

The third thing on my list is loss of purity. There ain't nothin' pure anymore. The food we eat today, the clothes we wear. Everything is chemicals. Synthetic. It's not natural no more.

It's not like the old times when everything was made from scratch. People put workmanship into the things they sold. There is no fuckin' craftsmanship left in the fuckin' world today. Today everything is made in fuckin' China.

Manufacturers are all on the fuckin' cheap. Not that things are fuckin' cheap to buy. They cost an arm and a leg. They're just cheaply made. Everywhere you're getting ripped off, because the motherfuckers who are making and selling the crap are overwhelmed by fuckin' greed.

You used to eat chicken and you were eating fucking chicken. Now you eat chicken and you're eating the fuckin' growth steroids. It gets to the point where you don't even want to eat these fuckin' things no more. Who the fuck knows what they put in them?

Number four on my list of things that piss me off most of all is the kids today. The world is fuckin' filled with very lazy kids today just sittin' on their asses. They don't like to work.

They press a fuckin' button and they want thirty dollars an hour. They don't like to work with their hands. That bothers me. You know who I blame? The fuckin' parents. My kid, he would be out there breakin' stones. That would teach him how to make the fuckin' money. You don't get it for nothin'. You got to learn how to do it.

I know, I know. A lot of it is because people have fuckin' money today. Some of the people do. The ones that don't are hungry. The others they got money and they're fuckin' lazy. Nobody wants to lift a fuckin' finger. They just sit there. "Oh, a lightbulb has fuckin' blown, I think I'll call a fuckin' guy to replace it." Lazy bastards, the ones with money.

All that money, it's good and it's bad. My first car cost fifteen dollars. I bought an old jalopy, a '55 Olds. I bought it out of the junkyard. Lasted me about three months. Then I got a '49 Olds coupe, ran like a top. Only one night I was coming home and there was a divider in the street. I didn't see it. I went over the divider and broke the rear axle. Point is, everything I ever got I worked for. I paid my fuckin' dues.

Today, the parents buy the kids new cars. A kid driving a brand-new car in high school? What do the parents think? Do they think they're doing him some fuckin' good? The kids says, "Fuck it, if the car breaks down, or I fuckin' total it, my parents'll just buy me a new one!" Let'em go out and fuckin' earn it. That's what I say.

I didn't have no fuckin' rich parents to say, "Here's your rent money. Here's your car. Here's your insurance. Here's your fuckin' meal money."

Me, I did it on my own.

38. Losing a Million Bucks

People hear my story and they want to know: "Big Mike, how do you lose a fuckin' million dollars?"

Let me tell you here and now, a million dollars is piss water. You can go through that in fuckin' three months. Money, when you're a fuckin' mess, is like water. It slips through your fuckin' fingers.

I was drinkin' and I was druggin'. That was the one problem. That leads to a whole fuckin' series of bad decisions. The domino effect as it applies to self-destruction. Your judgment gets very bad.

You know how you try calling a flip of a coin, if you do it enough you'll be right half the time and wrong half the time? With drinkin' and druggin', you call the flip of the coin wrong every fuckin' time.

You go out and pay top dollar to buy things that are fuckin' boring by the time you get 'em home and they end up in the fuckin' closet. Pretty soon you don't have a million dollars anymore, instead you got a closet full of shit.

I bought a car. Top dollar. It was a Blazer. The very first day, I backed it up and I dented it. I brought it back to the guy and told him to sell me a new one. That's how crazy I was. It wasn't even a big fuckin' dent. I was out of my fuckin' mind.

Obviously if I was straight I would never have done that. I would just have had the dent fixed. So you see, I could flip the coin again and again, but I was never going to get it right. Not even by accident.

Poker? Fuggedabouddit. The racetrack? It got so bad I wasn't just picking losers, I was picking the ponies that broke down or got confused and ran the wrong fuckin' way.

I would go out and buy all kinds of shit. That's what you do when you are under the influence. I would go out and party my fuckin' face off, very fuckin' night. When I went out to eat, I picked up everybody's check. You can go through a million dollars pretty fuckin' quick.

You know that Frank Sinatra song, "That's Life"? That's me. Ridin' high in April, fuckin' shot down in May. I've seen the fuckin' mountaintop and I've scraped fuckin' bottom. I was a millionaire, lost all my money, and ended up in a homeless shelter. I'd left Brooklyn at this point and was living in Fairfield, Connecticut.

And the fall from the top wasn't gradual, either. It was a free fall, and when I crashed I crashed hard. How does a guy have everything and then blow it? Well, it was a combination of factors, none of them good. Bottom line, I blew every dime.

I got in trouble at the shelter. There was a guy there, a smart aleck if there ever was one. At dinner one night he cursed my mother.

He said, "Your mother sucks big elephant dicks."

I grabbed him and took him outside.

I hit him with a bat over the head. True story. They threw me out of the shelter. The official reason was because I hit the guy on shelter property. I slept in my car, a Dodge Colt!—for seven months, with a dog. I had a little beagle. I had to take a shower at the YMCA. I was still drinkin' and druggin'. I didn't start my comeback until I cut that shit out.

So, my story goes from one extreme to the other. I started all over again. It's a tough thing to do, because once you go dead nobody wants you. Like millions before me, I didn't see the error of my ways and get off all that crap until I hit bottom. I guess it's because when you hit bottom, you got no choice. If you can't swallow without puking and you're a fuckin' vagrant on the street, you can't buy booze. You can't buy dope.

The first part of the fucking detox goes down on the street or maybe a fuckin' jail cell. By the time a doctor sees you, he's too fuckin' late. After that it's just a matter of staying clean.

Me, I used fear of embarassment as a way to stay

I've seen the fuckin' mountain-top and I've scraped fuckin' bottom. I was a millionaire, lost all my money, and ended up on the street.

sober. I found the way I got when I was fucked up embarrassing, and I didn't want to be that way no more.

When you're in the street and you got no place to sleep, and you ain't got ten cents in your pocket to put toward a bottle of whiskey, you're in fuckin' trouble. I went into the shelter.

I was there about a year. It was a terrible experience. You don't wanna be there but you gotta be there so what are ya gonna do? No more drinkin' no more druggin'. Sober. Now the only addiction I got left is food.

My comeback started in the street. I started out in

the street and my comeback began in the street, too. I was thinking straight for the first time in years and that helped a lot. There was a fuckin' adjustment period, though. Like sobriety was the new fuckin' drug and I had to get used to it, had to get used to the new head. After years at sea I had to get my fuckin' land legs back. But I did, and I've kept my fuckin' head screwed on straight ever since.

After I got my head together I had to get my business back. Tougher than you might think. I had no capital. No backers. I had to start from scratch, to start with nothing and build it into something.

I started hustling tickets again, the U.S. Open tennis, Shea, Yankee Stadium, the Garden, Radio fuckin' City for the fuckin' Rockettes. If it was a hot ticket, I made sure I had some. Little by little, I built it up.

Every week I would make four, five hundred and I would invest it. I'd use the money to buy more tickets and pretty soon I was making a thousand a week. And so on. I don't know how the fuck I did it. God only knows.

39. The United Fuckin' Nations

The United Nations is a useless piece of shit. It serves no purpose. It's just there for monetary reasons, to give people fuckin' jobs. They never get nothin' accomplished in the UN.

Nobody listens to the fuckin' UN, and nobody listens to each other inside the UN, you see these diplomats with earphones on. I think they're listening to Pink

Floyd. I think they're listening to fuckin' "Dark Side of the Moon."

So what the fuck do you need the United Nations for? If it was up to me, I'd put in condos and kick all those chiseling, anti-American diplomats out of the country. But only after they paid all them parking tickets.

40. Reality TV Sucks

I fuckin' hate reality TV. I think it's the most horrible thing I ever saw in my fucking life. The things that people'll do. Just to go on fuckin' television and win fucking money.

Reality TV sucks. Pizza is good. (Photo courtesy Kevin Helmick)

The fuckin' TV people, they don't want you to be happy.

Happy fuckin' people don't watch TV, see the commercials, buy the fuckin' product.

People wake up and they're fuckin' depressed every day. TV teaches us that people will humiliate themelves beyond repair in exchange for a thousand dollars. No, to tell the truth, you wouldn't even need the thousand dollars. They'll humiliate themselves in exchange for five minutes on TV.

If you put an ad in the newspaper tomorrow that said, "We want to buy your soul for a thousand dollars," do you know how many souls they would have at the end

> *People will do anything for money. Anything. And if we ever had any doubts that that was true, reality television proves it.*

of the fuckin' day? People would give it right up. "Here's my fuckin' soul. Where's the cash?"

People will do anything for money. Anything. And if we ever had any doubts that that was true, reality television proves it. If they wanted to have a reality show, we want to come into your house, into your fuckin' bedroom and watch you have sex with a fuckin' goat, they would have twenty million people volunteering.

Money and fame. Money or fame. People'll do anything. And yet people like these reality shows. I can't stand 'em.

The one I watched the longest and that was only because I couldn't believe how fuckin' bad it was, was *The Apprentice*, with that fuckin' Donald Trump. First of all, I can't stand the rat bastard. Donald Trump is a phony bastard and I can't look at his fucking face.

Then they had that fuckin' show *Survivor*, where the people eat snakes and rats. They got one show where they try to get all of the contestants to throw up, by eating monkey guts or some fuckin' thing. If you don't throw up you win the round—and lose your fucking soul!

They send these people through fucking jungles. I mean, what's on these people's mind? They do it for the fame and the money. They will lie and cheat and steal for a rat's ass full of fame. That's the kind of fuckin' world you live in today.

They rob their own mother. They rob their own father. Sisters, brothers, friends, it don't make no fuckin' difference to these fuckin' people. They steal the fuckin' teeth out of their grandmother's mouth.

There's no honor anymore. It doesn't make any difference to these fuckin' people. It's like they are fucking missing the part of us that makes us fuckin' human. They lack fuckin' integrity.

41. Bill and Hill

If I had to make a bet, and I'm a gambler, if I put up on the board in Vegas, "Do Bill Clinton and Hillary Clinton sleep in the same bed?" I would make it five-

> *Clinton should have fuckin' bragged about it:* "*I am the leader of the fuckin' free world and I'll get a blow job whenever and wherever I want.*"

hundred-to-one odds they don't. A thousand to one, you get they don't sleep in the same room.

It ain't just Clinton. It's the Republicans, too. These guys, they don't fuckin' sleep with their wives. They go with high-price hookers. When they get caught, they say they were fuckin' drunk. That's all. They say they were on fuckin' narcotics. They go into rehab.

Speaking of Bill Clinton, Bill Clinton is one of the smartest guys I ever seen in my life. He's a con artist. He's the world's number one flimflam man. You got to admire a fuckin' guy like that. "I did not have sex with that woman." He lied in front of a congressional committee. You or me, we'd be doing time for perjury if we fuckin' tried to pull that shit. Bill Clinton skates. He's a fucking genius.

And he still gets a fucking pension. I mean, if you're impeached, how can you get a fucking pension? He gets Secret Service the rest of his fucking life. He's goin' around getting a hundred thousand fuckin' dollars a speech.

The American people must be idiots. How can you believe one fuckin' word this guy says? He couldn't even admit he was getting his fuckin' twizzler toked on by that chubby intern, Monica Lewinsky.

Clinton should have fuckin' bragged about it: "I am the leader of the fuckin' free world and I'll get a blow job whenever and wherever I want. Fuck you self-righteous assholes who don't approve."

That's what he should have said. Be a fucking man. Fess up. But he fuckin' lied and that made him the fuckin' asshole. If Hillary gets elected president can you imagine Bill following her around, trying to get the fuckin' stick out of her ass! That would be a fuckin' riot.

And the Secret Service, I'd tell them that I needed to get the scoop. I'd give them $100,000 if they'd answer one fucking question: Are Bill and Hill fuckin' sleepin' in the same room at night? No way. She hasn't gotten fucked in years. Sex ain't her thing. It's power that turns her on.

That's John "Johnny Farts" Farta in the white T-shirt, standing with Louie Cantarella on the corner of Liberty Avenue and Chestnut Street. With a name like Johnny Farta, he learned to defend himself pretty damn quick. (Photo courtesy Brian Merlis, www.brooklynpix.com)

42. With a Name Like Johnny Farta, You're Gonna Have Problems

John Anthony Farta was a guy from our neighborhood, lived over on Carlton Avenue. His parents were first-generation wops, didn't speak much English. That was pretty common back then.

Naturally, we called him Johnny Farts, 'cause with a name like Farta, it would almost have been a sin not to. Johnny hated being called Johnny Farts and who could really blame him. He would swear on a stack of fuckin' Bibles that his family's real name was Fartamigliatto, that some schmucko at Ellis Island shortened it to Farta when his folks came over from Sicily. Maybe the guy at Ellis Island thought it was just funny, or maybe he couldn't spell Fartamigliatto (and who could?) and it was easier to just shorten it to Farta. Or maybe the guy's wife wouldn't come across the night before and he was in a pissed-off mood. Whatever the reason, Farta it became and Farta it stayed.

Johnny was a pretty nice guy—with a name like Farta, it didn't pay to be a prick. A lot of guys would've turned mean getting called Johnny Farts their whole lives. Johnny Farta tried to take the constant ribbing in stride, but there was one problem: Johnny Farts lived up to his name. He farted all the fuckin' time.

Like you'd be sitting in the tenth row of the Brooklyn Paramount and you'd hear *pffft pfft pfffft* and you'd know Johnny Farts had just strolled in. (If the actual sound didn't tip you off, the smell of eggplant parmigiana would, usually within two minutes.) In fact, his whole family farted up a storm—his mother, father, and little sister Angelina. She got the nickname "the Little Bombardier" 'cause she could outfart the rest of her family. Was it too much garlic in Mrs. Farta's cooking? Could've been. All I remember is, when the Fartas came down the street, you crossed to the other side.

At Sunday morning mass at St. Bernadette's, they had the whole pew to themselves. Hell, the Fartas gave new meaning to the word *pew.*

Halfway through fifth grade, a new kid came into our class, a big, fat, freckle-faced Irisher named Georgie O'Looney. Mean-spirited little bastard. When the teacher took attendance that morning, O'Looney heard her say "John Farta" and he started cackling, elbowing me in the ribs and saying, "John Farta—that's a funny name."

No shit, Sherlock. We'd known Johnny Farts since fuckin' kindergarten.

Johnny glared at Georgie O'Looney and shot him the

Johnny was a pretty nice guy—with a name like Farta, it didn't pay to be a prick.

bird. O'Looney whispered to him, "I'm gonna kick your fuckin' ass, greaseball."

The challenge was thrown down and no way could Johnny Farts back away. What Georgie O'Looney didn't know, however, was that, even though he was a scrawny kid and looked like a pushover, Johnny could take care of himself in a brawl. He'd plenty of experience, always defending the family name. I mean, he was no fuckin' Sonny Liston but he could give as good as he got even when his opponents—like O'Looney—were bigger.

Recess comes and Georgie O'Looney goes right for Johnny in the playground. He had three inches and twenty pounds on Johnny and it's likely he came from a long line of Irish bullies.

O'Looney starts swinging his arms like fuckin' King Kong and charges Johnny full throttle. They go flying into the dirt, wrestling around. O'Looney can't seem to get a grip on Johnny and it's pissing him off big time.

Johnny scrambles to his feet. O'Looney's still squirming around in the dirt, trying to find him. Johnny seizes the moment and kicks O'Looney hard right in the sweet-meats. Then Johnny boots O'Looney in the ass and sits on his head, his ass right on O'Looney's nose. The fun is about to begin.

Johnny's one of those lucky people who can fart at will. He grunts a couple of times and starts letting them rip, right up O'Looney's nostrils. O'Looney starts bellowing—having someone fart up his nose is a new experience.

"Say 'uncle,' you sheeney piece of shit, or I'll crap in your mouth," Johnny says.

O'Looney doesn't need a second warning. "Uncle, uncle!" he screams. Johnny gets up and gives O'Looney one last kick in the head for good measure. The Irisher stands up and wipes his nose, hanging his head in shame. Sulking, he walks away, totally humiliated.

Johnny never had no trouble with him again.

The moral of the story is, never pick a fight with a kid who can fart up your nose.

43. Illegal Immigrants

So the Big Man was reading about all them illegal Mexicans protesting around the country to become legal residents of the United States. And a bunch of 'em were rioting and a dozen cops were injured. Way to go, guys— you ain't gonna get much sympathy from us, pulling that shit. Then again, this was in L.A., and that cesspool's already been taken over by them Mexican gangs.

The Big Man got nothing against immigrants—hell, my people were immigrants and 99 percent of everyone in America comes from immigrants.

But these Mexicans are acting like it's their right to become U.S. citizens and the Big Man is here to tell you that's bullshit.

For one thing, they won't learn English so everything has to be in English and Spanish. Shit, you go to a fuckin' ATM and you gotta choose. Or else, call a business and you get, "Press one for English, press two for Spanish."

What kinda shit is that? Time was, everyone who came to America learned English—and was proud to do it.

For Chrissake, I see them Puerto Ricans driving around with them PR flags on their dashboard or hanging from their rearview mirrors, and it pisses me off. They should be sporting American flags! They like Puerto Rico such damn much, let 'em go back.

There's like thirty million illegal aliens in the United States and we deport maybe 2 percent of 'em. I blame the politicians in Washington, those sons of whores. The Democraps and the Republicans—they're all the same bunch of useless bums. They don't give a shit if some Crips or Bloods do a home invasion—they just wanna legalize them so they can get more votes.

Vote for the Big Man in 2008! If I become president, I'll build a wall between us and Mexico and fill the Rio Grande with battery acid so they can't cross over.

I take an oath on my mother—you wanna get rid of all thirty million of them illegals in five minutes? It's easy—just tell 'em we found 'em jobs and watch how fast they tear ass back to Mexico.

Anyway, think about it.

44. Flag-Desecrating Islamic Militants

You see the fuckin' news the other day? Here in New York, they got some Islamic militants staging a fuckin' protest. They got the American flag on the floor, Ol' Glory on the fuckin' floor.

Back in my day, you had to burn a flag if it touched the floor. That was what you did, out of respect. If the flag touched the ground or the floor you had to burn it, in a fucking ceremony.

These Islamic assholes are using the fuckin' Stars and Stripes for a fuckin' rug. They're steppin' on it, rippin' it up. They say they are representing Islam and that the United States is no fucking good.

Back in my day in Brooklyn, if they had did that, there'd be six fuckin' dead bodies layin' there.

Back in my day in Brooklyn, if they had did that, there'd be six fuckin' dead bodies layin' there. They would have been layin' right on the fuckin' ground. But today they allow that.

You can use the American flag for a rug in public—as long as you have the fuckin' correct permits. I wouldn't give a fuck what they had. If they picked the wrong neighborhood to do that in Brooklyn, they'd carry all fuckin' six of 'em away in fuckin' wooden boxes. That's what they would do.

You see what happened to fuckin' Al Sharpton when he went to Bensonhurst, Brooklyn, to march in an Italian neighborhood? He got stabbed—another half inch, he'd be dead. There are certain sections of Brooklyn you don't wanna march through. There are certain people you can't fuck with.

It's only common sense. I wouldn't go up to Harlem and march down the middle of the street sayin' the blacks are no fuckin' good. How long would I last, sayin' that shit on a fuckin' street corner outside the fuckin' Apollo on fuckin' 125th Street?

People can think whatever they want and they can say whatever they want. We got fuckin' freedom of speech in this country, but if you go to the other guy's neighborhood and start to scream that he's no fuckin' good, then you got to be smart enough to know there's gonna be trouble.

It goes both ways. There's gonna be fuckin' trouble if you try shit like that. But the flag-desecrating Islamic militants are fuckin' getting a pass. For now.

45. Airlines Today

The airlines of today are not like the airlines of yesterday. When I flew first class years ago, the seats were three times the size they are today. They served filet mignon. Lobster tails. Prime rib.

First class was fuckin' first class. You would get ice-cream sundaes for dessert. Today, the seats in first class are just a fraction of an inch bigger than the seats in coach, not much bigger.

And they give you a bag of peanuts and a fuckin' dried-out fuckin' turkey sandwich. What is the purpose

> *Can you fit in a fuckin' air-plane bathroom? I can't. I try to take a shit in one of them fuckin' things and my knees hit the fuckin' wall.*

of flying first class if the seats are only a smidgen bigger and you still get the dried-up fucking turkey sandwich?

I don't want the bag of nuts. I am flying first class because I want to be catered to. I want to be wined and dined. That's why I'm paying the fifteen hundred one way to go to fuckin' Florida.

For that kind of fuckin' money I want to get a first-class experience, so that I'll go out and tell people, "Oh man, that American Airlines, they wined and dined me. I had prime rib of beef. Filet mignon. Lobster tails. The beautiful stewardess made me a big fuckin' ice-cream sundae. Fresh. Whipped cream. All the champagne I want. The seats were huge. I stretched out. I was watching all the fuckin' TV channels, makin' telephone calls for free, using the plane phone there." That's what you want to be able to tell people. Instead, a dried-up fuckin' turkey sandwich. If I'd known this was the fucking case, I'd've just drove down there.

And the bathrooms. Can you fit in a fuckin' airplane bathroom? I can't. I try to take a shit in one of them fuckin' things and my knees hit the fuckin' wall. And you got couples having sex in those little bathrooms.

46. Condoms

I guess if I wasn't married to Mona and the Big Man was still playing the fuckin' field, I'd wear a fuckin' condom. There's some scary shit out there today, so you got to be fuckin' careful.

But when I was a young man, I didn't use 'em. I never wore a fuckin' condom. And I never caught no fuckin' diseases, neither. It's just a matter of where you stick your carrot. Either the honey pot is good or the honey pot is fuckin' bad. Luck of the fuckin' draw.

It's all different today. The young people today are

very sexually promiscuous. It ain't like years ago. Today, it's a normal thing for a thirteen-, fourteen-year-old-girl to have sex. The parents encourage it.

Today, the teenaged girls get a prescription for birth-control pills. It's the fuckin' age. We're in a sexual society. So today, the young people, male and female, they've got to protect themselves.

You don't know who these people have slept with. Today, the girls, they'll sleep with you on the first date. It's not like when I was a fuckin' kid and you had to take 'em out three, four times.

And even then sometimes you wouldn't get any pussy. You'd get to the fuckin' third date and all you'd get was a hand job. Sometimes you got laid on the first date, but that was only sometimes. It wasn't like today.

Either the honey pot is good or the honey pot is fuckin' bad. Luck of the fuckin' draw.

47. Richie the Retard Gets Laid (Well, Almost)

When the Big Man was a kid, we used to call mental retards "mongoloids," 'cause they looked like them Asian Mongols from the Flash Gordon movies. But today it's not politically correct to say that, so the expression is "Down syndrome." Shit, you're not even allowed to say "retard" anymore—today it's "mentally challenged."

> *Shit, you're not even allowed to say "retard" anymore—today it's "mentally challenged." This PC crap is taking all the fun out of everything. What's next—we gonna start calling women "Vaginal Americans"?*

What's wrong with saying just "retard"? It's a lot easier to remember.

Listen to the Big Man: this PC crap is taking all the fun out of everything. What's next—we gonna start calling women "Vaginal Americans"?

Every neighborhood in New York City has their own local retard, a modern-day equivalent of the village idiot. Our retard was Richie Paluso. Richie the Retard, we called him, 'cause he was soft in the head. He wasn't a mongoloid but he was definitely a retard. I mean, shit, you don't repeat second grade five times if you're not a couple of french fries short of a cheeseburger deluxe. It got to the point where he was twice the size of the other kids in his class and kept falling off the little wooden chair at his desk. It was cheaper for the NY Board of Education to give him the boot than to order a bigger chair.

For another thing, who else would trade you a dime for a penny and be happy about it? Like, you'd go up to Richie and say, "Hey, Richie, look, my penny's bigger than your dime. Wanna swap?" And he would. When you're a retard, it's all about size. The gag worked twice as good when you were swapping Richie nickels for dimes. But then you were looking at a smaller profit margin.

Richie was already seventeen or eighteen when I first

This is Delfina "Delfi" Tortorro, who Lenny Cantalupo almost tricked into schtupping Richie the Retard. (Photo courtesy Brian Merlis, www.brooklynpix.com)

remember seeing him. He lived with his Uncle Momo in a small apartment over Noodleman's tailor shop on Glenwood Road. He did odd jobs around the neighborhood, making deliveries for Schwindenhamer's deli and Pop Majeski's newsstand, always pulling that Radio Flyer wagon of his. He was tall and skinny and, if you closed one eye and squinted the other, you could even say he looked almost normal. If Anthony Perkins drooled and had the mind of an eight-year-old, he could've played Richie in a movie.

One afternoon in July, a bunch of us were all hanging out on Bobo Mangano's stoop. Me, Little Farfel Cohen, Charlie "the Bug" Nitzberg, and Lenny Cantelupo, Junior. We were trying to decide how to beat the heat, either the movies or maybe Coney Island, when along came Richie the Retard, pulling that battered red wagon. It was loaded with empty Orange Crush soda bottles. He was heading over to Majeski's, where he got a penny apiece on the deposit. They were actually worth three cents a bottle, but Majeski thought it was okay to chisel poor Richie because he was a retard and would never know the difference.

Watching him go by, Little Farfel said, "Hey, you think Richie the Retard's ever been laid?"

Most of us, at the time, were fifteen, sixteen, and I don't think any of us had ever gotten laid, either. Not that we would admit it—to hear us tell it, we were all Errol fuckin' Flynn. But that wasn't the point. Someday we'd get laid. The outlook for Richie wasn't that bright.

"Richie the Retard getting laid?" Bobo asked. "I don't think he even knows how to choke his fuckin' chicken."

"Yeah," Charlie the Bug chimed in. "What broad would give that big 'tard a tumble?"

That's when Lenny Junior piped up, "I know someone who will."

Our pal Lenny Junior's old man was Leonard "the Undertaker" Cantalupo, one of Tommy "the Mayor" Funzi's most trusted capos. Tommy Funzi was the unofficial mayor of Canarsie, meaning he ran all the rackets in the neighborhood and had a crew of, like, twenty-five wiseguys working under him. Leonard the Undertaker was Tommy Funzi's best torpedo and a man feared by everyone on Rockaway Parkway. The old Italian ladies on the block used to cross themselves when he passed by.

So Lenny Junior, being the son of Leonard the Undertaker, naturally became the leader of our gang. We all deferred to him on matters such as sex because unlike the rest of us, Lenny Junior got laid all the time. He wasn't really good looking but the broads were attracted to him 'cause his dad was a hit man. Women. Try to figure them.

Lenny Junior was giving it some serious thinking. He said, "I think Delfi would fuck the retard."

"Delfi?" Charlie the Bug asked. (He got that name 'cause he liked to fry ants on the sidewalk with a magnifying glass.) "Your Delfi?"

Lenny Junior said, "How many fuckin' Delfis have you seen me with, asshole?"

I had to say something because I could see Lenny Junior was warming to the idea real quick and I smelled disaster. I said, "I dunno. Ain't that kinda cruel, settin' him up with Delfi? I mean, what Richie the Retard don't know about sex is a lot."

"He's gotta learn sometime," Lenny Junior said. "And shit, how would youse guys like to go through life never gettin' any pussy?"

He had a point.

Delfina "Delfi" Tortorro was Lenny Junior's on again/off again girlfriend. ("I get on her and when I'm done, I get offa her," Lenny Junior said.) She was a little older than us, twenty or twenty-one, and lived on East 98th Street with her widowed mother, an incredibly fat, foul-tempered woman who screamed in Italian if you stepped within two feet of her postage stamp–size front lawn. (The joke about her was, "What's the difference between an elephant and Delfi Tortorro's old lady? A mustache and a black housedress.")

Delfi wasn't much better in the disposition department—she was one of them high-strung, shrill Brooklyn babes with two-inch fingernails she painted purple. Like most Brooklyn broads, she wore a lot of makeup—I think she plastered that shit on with a fuckin' cake decorator—to cover up her acne scars. She kept her hair in one them beehive hairdos big enough for a fuckin' pterodactyl to build a nest in. She did have the best tits on East 98th Street, though, I'll give her that.

Lenny Junior went around with her when he was be-tween real girlfriends, saying, "I only bang her when I'm mad at my dick for something." The word around Canarsie was, Delfi got really bad migraine headaches if she didn't have sex two or three times a day. Me, I thought that story was bullshit—I think Delfi was one of them nymphomaniacals. When she was horny, which was most of the time, she wasn't too picky about her sex partners. If a guy wasn't available at those moments,

Lenny Junior swore, certain vegetables would be sub-
stituted for the real thing. ("Every time I walk past a
fuckin' salad," Lenny Junior said, "I break into a cold
sweat.")

For some reason though, she only liked older guys,
which left me and my pals out in the cold. (Lenny Junior was the exception.) Little Farfel Cohen tried once
and Defli told him, "Go home, you little twerp. You'd
fall in."

The best time to approach Delfi was around 9:00 A.M.
when her mother went off to morning Mass at St. Bernadette's, which she did every day without fail. Then she'd
spend another hour confessing her sins to Father Anthony
(or "Fadda Antinny" in Brooklynese), who rarely looked
up from his Mickey Spillane paperback while she droned
on. He'd give her 150 Hail Marys and 200 Our Fathers—
pretty harsh. But it wasn't because the old lady had sinned.
He punished her for boring him shitless.

After Mass, she'd trudge over to Mr. Grippo's fruit and
vegetable market and pinch all the honeydews and pears
and tomatoes (which drove poor Grippo up the fuckin'
wall) and then complain that they were too mushy and
he should charge her less. They'd end up bellowing Italian curses at each other. She'd call Grippo *"testa di merda"*
("shithead") and he'd say to her, *"Non mi scazzare i
coglioni"* ("Don't bust my balls").

After one particularly nasty encounter, Grippo picked
up the biggest cucumber in his store and said, "Take-a
this home as a gift for-a your daughter, Delfina."

"My Delfina no like-a the cucumber," Mama Tortorro
said.

"I heard-a different," Grippo said.

So between Hail Marying and squeezing Grippo's melons, old Mama Tortorro could be counted on to be out of the house for at least a couple of hours, more than enough time to slip in and jump Delfi's bones. Twice, if a guy was extra horny.

Anyway, Lenny Junior said, "I'll go up to Delfi's tomorrow when her old cow of a mother is at Mass. Then one of youse calls Schwindenhamer's and ask him to send Richie over with some soda and baloney sandwiches. Once he's inside the house, I'll handle the rest."

"How do youse know she'll do it with Richie?" Charlie the Bug wanted to know. "Maybe she won't wanna ball no retard."

Lenny Junior was way ahead of us. He said, "She ain't gonna know it's Richie."

"Whaddaya mean?" Bobo asked, puzzled as the rest of us.

"The minute her old lady leaves, Delfi's gonna get one of her headaches—happens like fuckin' clockwork. Her bedroom faces the brick wall of the Antonucci place next door. When you yank down the shade, the room gets blacker than Aunt Jemima's asshole. I'll get her all hot and horny, you know, squeeze her nips. Then, when Richie rings the doorbell downstairs, I'll tell him that Delfi's got his money and to go up there and collect it. She'll be so sexed up by then she'll jump his bones and won't even know the difference."

I still wasn't sure—the whole setup sounded pretty half-assed to me. What's that expression, the best-laid plans of mice and men? As things turned out, nobody got laid that day. Well, maybe the mice. But no men.

The next morning, at 8:30 A.M., we tossed a coin to see who'd call Schwindenhamer's deli. I lost.

He answered on the second ring. "Yah, Schwinden-hamer's Delicatessen, haloo?"

Mr. Schwindenhamer always sounded a little guarded when he answered his phone, probably because every third call was from some smart-ass who said stuff like, "Bring me two purple tits on rye, you Nazi cocksucker." This pissed Karl Schwindenhamer off something fierce, not because of the crack itself but because he was Dutch and hated the fuckin' Nazis more than anyone.

So I placed the order for half a dozen baloney sand-wiches and eight bottles of Boylan's root beer to be de-livered to Delfi's house on East 98th and to have it there in half an hour. Since me and the other guys would most likely be eating the sandwiches ourselves, Bobo whis-pered, "I want mine with mayo, on whole wheat." Little Farfel and Charlie the Bug wanted theirs on rye with mustard. I told them all to shut the fuck up 'cause they were making me all confused.

Lenny Junior, meanwhile, was across the street from Delfi's house, crouched behind some bushes, waiting for her mother to leave. Sure enough, at a quarter to nine, out came Mama Tortorro, who immediately started yelling at a cocker spaniel that was pissing on her lawn.

"Give me two purple tits on rye, you Nazi cocksucker."

"*Vaffanculo!* (fuck you)," she screamed at the dog, then went on her way. For good measure, the dog crapped on the sidewalk in front of her house.

Lenny Junior waited until she was around the corner and out of sight, then dashed across East 98th Street and knocked on the door. Delfi opened it and she was wearing a pink bathrobe with nothing on underneath. She was ready for action, any action. You got to understand that Lenny ain't the only one who's dipping his wick into her. The mailman, the meter reader from Brooklyn Gas, assorted delivery boys, and even the Jehovah's Witness guy who went around giving out those Bible pamphlets had all, at one time or another, torn off a nice piece of Delfi's action. This morning, however, the early bird got the worm. That worm being Lenny Junior.

"Well, well, look who's got a chubby," Delfi said, puffing on a Parliament. She was mad at Lenny Junior 'cause she heard he'd taken Heidi Hillfinger to see *The Great Escape* at the Loew's Oriental. "Whadda you want?"

"Ain't you gonna invite me in?" Lenny wanted to know. Delfi looked tense and pissed off, which meant she was having one of her headaches. Which also meant she was hornier than a merchant marine after six months at sea.

"Why should I?" Delfi asked. "You just wanna boff me and run. Why don't you go get Heidi Hillfinger to spread for you?"

"Aw, c'mon, Delfi," he said. "You know Heidi don't mean shit to me."

Lenny Junior took her anger in stride. He knew Delfi was just busting his chops 'cause she could. Not to mention, when it came to chicks, Lenny Junior was slicker than snot on a doorknob. He could sweet-talk a fuckin' mother superior into giving him a blow job. Lenny turned on the old Cantalupo charm, whispering sweet nothings in her ear and squeezing her ass under the bathrobe. Delfi melted like a cheese sandwich on Midnight Sadie's luncheonette grill. She dropped her robe on the kitchen floor and led him upstairs to her bedroom.

Around the same time, we saw Richie the Retard come out of Schwindenhamer's, pulling that stupid red wagon.

So me and Bobo, Little Farfel, and Charlie the Bug joined up with him. Little Farfel said, "Hey, whassup, Richie?"

"I'm makin' a da-rivery," Richie said.

"Yeah? Where?" Charlie the Bug asked, making conversation.

"Over there," Richie the Retard said, pointing to somewhere down the street. Fact was, the half-wit was walking in the opposite direction of the Tortorro house. Richie got lost pretty easy. Why Schwindenhamer even trusted the idiot is beyond me. Like the time Richie was supposed to make a delivery to a house on Avenue L— two fuckin' blocks from Schwindenhamer's—and walked all the way to Brownsville in that perpetual retard fog before realizing he had no fuckin' idea where he was. He sat on the curb and cried until a cop took pity on him and drove him back to Canarsie in a squad car. It was the most fuckin' exciting day he'd had since he fell off the flying elephant ride at Coney Island.

Its being our job to make sure Richie got to where he was supposed to be, Charlie the Bug asked, "Ain't Delfi's house the other way?"

"Yeah," Little Farfel said. "I think you're going wrong." Under his breath, he added, "Ya dumb fuckin' moron."

I could see that Richie's brain circuits were on fuckin' overload—questions in general, even easy ones like "What's your name?" made Richie all *farblonjet*, crazy in the head.

And of course, it never occurred to him to even ask how we knew where he was headed. That's a retard for you.

I motioned to Bobo, who nodded and motioned to Little Farfel and Charlie the Bug. I put my arm around Richie's shoulder and led him away from the others, saying, "Hey, Richie, I want you to see this."

I pulled a bent nickel out of my pocket and showed it to him. Richie said, "It looks like a money."

"It's a nickel," I said. "A magic nickel."

Richie's eyes brightened. "Yeah?"

"Yup," I said. "All youse got to do is rub it three times and your wish will come true."

You may have guessed that I was making all this shit up as I went along. Behind us, Bobo, Little Farfel, and Charlie the Bug were turning Richie's wagon around so Richie would pull it in the right fuckin' direction.

Richie started rubbing the nickel like he was trying to start a fuckin' campfire, his eyes shut tight. He was saying, "I wish I had a little pussy . . . I wish I had a little pussy . . ."

I take an oath to my mother, what happened next is no bullshit. Me and the other guys just looked at each other as if to say, "He wants *what?*" Then Richie opened his eyes and at that moment a small black cat darted out of an alley between Callahan's poolroom and the

Chinese laundry. Richie cried out, "Look—a little pussy! My wish came true."

The black cat ran right past us and of course Richie started chasing after him. None of us were superstitious guys but this was just too weird. Even Charlie the Bug, who was the biggest skeptic in our gang, said, "I think this shit is jinxed."

It was too late to turn back, though—Lenny Junior would've kicked the shit out of us for fucking everything up. So we all chasing after Richie, who was on his hands and knees trying to coax the cat out from under Porky Porcanetti's '59 Studebaker. We dragged him screaming at the top of his retarded lungs, "Richie wants a little pussy!"

Little Farfel said, "That's exactly what you're gonna get, Richie."

We guided him over to Delfi's house on East 98th. Richie rang the doorbell. Then things started happening really fast.

Upstairs in her bedroom, Lenny Junior was kissing and fondling Delfi's monster tits. She was out of her head with lust, about to fuckin' explode. She wanted his pecker inside her really bad and started yanking on the zipper of his Levi's, trying to unleash the beast. At this point, Lenny Junior was pretty hot and heavy himself and almost forgot about Richie the Retard and the Big Plan, as it later came to be known. He had Delfi's panties halfway down her legs.

Then the doorbell rang.

"Shit!" Delfi snapped. "Who the fuck is that?"

Lenny Junior started to get off the bed and Delfi said, "Stay here. Whoever it is will go away if we don't answer."

"Or they might not," Lenny said. "Let me go down there and get rid of 'em."

Lenny Junior came bounding down the stairs and opened the door. Richie was holding the bag with the baloney sandwiches and the Boylan's root beer. We were all standing behind him.

"Da-rivery," Richie the Retard said, handing the bag to Lenny. "You owe me two dollars and twelve cents."

Lenny Junior said, "We gotta go upstairs and get your money." He slammed the door in our faces and led Richie up the stairs to Delfi's bedroom. The rest of us quietly snuck back into the house—I mean shit, we had a right to see how this was going to play out.

Lenny Junior and Richie the Retard were standing at the door to Delfi's room. Lenny said, "Go on in. She has your money. But don't say anything because she has a bad headache, *capisce?*"

Richie was a little confused—he rarely got invited into peoples' houses when he made deliveries, much less into a woman's bedroom. But he couldn't go back to Schwindenhamer without the money so he cautiously opened the bedroom door and went inside. Lenny Junior slipped in behind him.

The minute Lenny disappeared inside the bedroom, me and the others huddled outside the bedroom door, pushing each other out of the way to peek through the keyhole. We couldn't see shit.

Delfi's room was blacker than midnight so as far as she knew, it was Lenny coming in. She was laying on the bed, stark naked. She said, "It's about time. Now get the hell over here, you hot guinea stud."

Richie did as he was told, trying to feel his way toward her voice in the darkness. He bumped into a chair but made it over to the foot of the bed, remembering not to say anything 'cause of Delfi's headache. Delfi went right for Richie's pants and yanked them down to his ankles. She reached into his underpants and grabbed his pecker. Richie was scared shitless but it felt kind of nice, too, so he kept his mouth shut. His dick got harder than marble in, like, half a second. Delfi wrapped her fingers around his swollen pecker and was about to slide it into her mouth when we heard the front door open and then slam shut.

Now Richie, who was finally learning the true purpose of that thing between his legs, got really fuckin' excited and couldn't help himself. Bam—he fired his monster wad of love juice right into Delfi's face like a fuckin' bazooka shot.

"You filthy pig piece of shit!" Delfi cried out, indignant as all hell.

"Dela-fina, I'm-a home," we heard Mama Tortorro call from the kitchen, and we all tried to scatter like a bunch of cockroaches when the lights are turned on. As fate would have it, Father Anthony got busted the day before when the monsignor caught him in the confessional with his cock halfway up some altar boy's poopchute. So morning Mass was canceled and Mama came home earlier than expected.

Bobo and Little Farfel dove into the bathroom and slammed the door. Charlie the Bug and me tried to head in the other direction but in the confusion, ended up slamming into each other like the fuckin' Three Stooges. Mama Tortorro, not finding Delfi in the kitchen, came thundering up the stairs. She was clutching a huge carrot, saying, "Dela-fina, how-a come Mr. Grippo always wanna give-a you the vegetables?"

She saw me and Charlie the Bug trying to scamper away and started screaming. "Who are you? Why you inna my house?"

She flung open the door to Delfi's bedroom, flooding it with light, just as Lenny Junior had squirmed under Delfi's bed. For a second or two, she couldn't quite comprehend what she was seeing: Delfi on her knees, trying to wipe Richie the Retard's spunk out of her eyes, Richie still standing there, his pants around his ankles.

Delfi screamed at Richie, "Who the fuck are you?"

Richie's head was about to explode. He took one look at Mama Tortorro, and his cock, which had been standing at attention, fainted dead away and tried to crawl up into his sweetmeats.

"Figlio di puttana! caccati in mano e prenditi a schiaffi! a Napoli! faccia di merda!" the old bag bellowed, and went right for poor Richie, who was paralyzed with fear. Mrs. Tortorro started walloping him with the carrot and chasing him around the room. He tried to make it through the doorway, his pants still around his ankles, and fell flat on his face. The old lady tripped over him and collapsed onto the poor bastard like a sack of brass doorknobs, knocking the wind out of him. Richie started blubbering, managed to stand, and pulled his pants up. He dashed down the stairs and bolted through the front door and his pants fell down again. The last time we saw him, he was running balls-ass naked from the waist down with the old lady hot on his heels, brandishing the fuckin' carrot like it was a Louisville Slugger. For a fat old lady, she could move pretty good.

The rest of us figured now was as good a time as any to get the fuck out of there. The last thing I remember is the image of Delfi standing on her stoop in her bathrobe, screaming curses at Lenny Junior as he tore ass down East 98th half a block behind us.

I'd like to say the story has a happy ending but I'd be bullshitting if I did.

For one thing, Schwindenhamer fired Richie the Retard when he came back without the money (though the rest of us later chipped in and paid the deli man the $2.12. It was the least we could do—we *did* end up eating the baloney sandwiches, 'cause Little Farfel was smart enough to snatch the bag up as he ran out of Delfi's house). A week or two later, Richie's Uncle Momo sent Richie away to some home for retards in Far Rockaway and we never saw him again.

Then Mama Tortorro ended up going to the cops, claiming that Richie had raped her daughter and wanting to file charges. She never got any further than the desk sergeant, though, because Delfi's reputation was common knowledge around the 83rd Precinct. Shit, I wouldn't be surprised if she'd fucked half the beat cops in the station.

"Delfi always loved a guy in a uniform," Lenny Junior declared.

Lenny Junior ended going into the family business, but he never really got the hang of killing. He was found stuffed into the trunk of a Lincoln Town Car under the Brooklyn-Queens Expressway about ten years ago, with three bullets in his head. There was a note pinned to his shirt that read "Next time, whack the right pigeon, you *stoonad*."

The rest of us went our separate ways, as teenagers do. And Delfi? Her mama packed her off to a convent somewhere upstate near Buffalo, where it was hoped the cold weather would chill Delfi's hot blood.

The last thing I remember Lenny Junior saying was, "Delfi's in a fuckin' convent? I'm sure she'll make some candlestick real happy."

48. Hugo Chávez, the Gasoline Pimp

Hey, how about that fuckin' Hugo Chávez, that fuckin' dictator they got down there in Venezuela. He's not afraid to make a fuckin' asshole out of himself, is he. He got up in front of the United fuckin' Nations and started screaming "*el Diablo*," talkin' about that Bush.

I mean, come on, give me a fuckin' break. The guy's a fuckin' dictator! A dictator! The way that guy dresses up there, in his red shirt and red pants, he looked like a fuckin' pimp. Only a pimp dresses like that. That's what he is. A pimp.

Fuck you, you rat bastard Venezuelan.

That Chávez owns all the Citgos. They should kick all the fuckin' Citgos out of the fuckin' country. Tell him to take his fuckin' gasoline and go home. You can help by boycotting Citgo.

Do you know how many people he put in front of the firing squad, that rat-fucking bastard? And he's got the fucking balls to call Bush the fucking devil? Fuck you, Chávez. Fuh-uh-uh-uh-uck you!

Fuck you, you rat bastard Venezuelan son of a bitch. I hope you die of fucking cancer, you bastard. How can there be any justice when this cocksucker is one of the richest bastards in the whole fuckin' world.

If you got a fuckin' choice between a Citgo or a Hess or a Sunoco, don't stop at the Citgo. That'll teach the red-pants pimp bastard to call that Bush *el Diablo* in front of the whole fuckin' United Nations.

And President Bush! What about you? How come you don't get up in front of the whole United Nations and call this cocksucker a fuckin' pimp, because that's what he is, a fuckin' pimp. So, come on, Georgie. Show me you got some fuckin' balls.

Hugo Chávez is no fuckin' good. Fuck you, Chávez! Fuck you, Chávez. I'm an American! I'm fuckin' proud to be an American.

49. Sushi

You know about this Japanese fuckin' food called sushi? What it is, is fucking slabs of raw fish tied to globs of sticky rice with ribbons of seaweed. Ummmm, that's good eatin'. I don't fuckin' think so.

Now you can eat sushi if you fuckin' want to, and more power to ya. Maybe it's good for you and maybe it's filled with nineteen of the twenty fuckin' essential vitamins or whatever.

> *Raw fish tied to globs of sticky rice with ribbons of seaweed. Ummmm, that's good eatin'. I don't fuckin' think so.*

But you couldn't get me to eat sushi for all the tea in fuckin' China. Maybe you got to require a taste for it, but that ain't happenin' for me. Not in this fuckin' lifetime—which unless you believe in fuckin' reincarnation is the only fuckin' lifetime you got.

I like fish. Cooked. Not raw. The hell with it. I ain't gonna eat that garbage. You got some sushi give it to somebody else, not to me. Maybe I should go on a fuckin' sushi diet.

That would get me to lose weight. A diet where I was only allowed to eat sushi. I wonder how fuckin' hungry I'd have to fuckin' get before I could get a piece of raw fish down my throat without fucking gagging.

50. The Fights

Here's a sport that's been dragged down into the fucking dumpster since the days when I was a kid: boxing. Don King ruined it. Once it was the greatest sport on Earth; nights didn't get more exciting than fight night.

The greatest fight I ever saw, bar none, was Frazier-Ali I. Madison Square Garden. Back in those days the seats way up near the fuckin' roof, the nosebleed seats at the Garden, were painted blue, and everybody called them "the blues."

If you were going to be sitting in the blues you knew you were getting a fuckin' nosebleed. For the Frazier-Ali fight, the blues were sellin' at the box office for twenty bucks a pop.

By fight night, I was getting a thousand bucks each for the blue seats. You had to be fuckin' careful that night. If you pulled out a ticket that night on Seventh Avenue in front of the Garden, there were fifty people who were willing to stab you for it.

There were these four Texans who took me to the bank on the day of the fight. They gave me $4,000 for four thousand-dollar tickets. They had to go get the money in the bank so I went with them. That's how big that fight was.

There was a who's who there that night. Frank Sinatra, you name it, they were there. If they were an actor or an actress they were there. You'll never see a fight of that magnitude again.

And, and, after all that fucking hype, the fight lived up to it. It was the greatest fucking fight I ever saw. Both men had chins of fucking stone. Before the fight, Ali predicted a sixth-round knockout, but it wasn't to be.

Frazier had a sound strategy. Since Ali was so quick, he forgot about headhunting and concentrated on the fuckin' body. Don't make no difference how many sit-ups you do before the fight, you take enough shots to the gut and your fuckin' legs start to go.

Frazier wanted to chop Ali down like a big oak tree, and when the body was gone, then he would go for Ali's head. The strategy worked, but Frazier took a fuckin' bad beating in the process.

Smokin' Joe took a couple of shots to the head for every body shot he landed. Frazier got some of his best licks in early, dominating the third and fourth rounds, scoring heavily to the body, then, in the fourth round, hurting Ali with a clean shot to the head.

Ali could never keep his fuckin' mouth shut anyway and began to taunt Frazier, telling him that he wasn't hurt. Ali leaned on the ropes and covered up. He let Frazier wail away in a sort-of prototype of the fuckin' rope-a-dope.

Ali told Frazier to come hit him, and Frazier would wade in. Sometimes, Ali would rope-a-dope, and sometimes he'd come up firing, snapping Frazier's fuckin' head back.

Frazier never knew which way it would be, and Ali wouldn't stop playing the game, remaining on the ropes, slack-legged, waving like a fuckin' drunk man with his gloves for Frazier to come hit him.

In the fifth round, Frazier managed to turn the tables on Ali, who was showing signs that the body shots were taking their toll. Frazier kept his arms low, perhaps try-

ing to shake out some arm-weariness, and invited Ali to
hit him.

Ali tried and missed several times, causing Frazier to
do the taunting for a time. At the end of the fifth round,
Frazier patted Ali on top of the head. After three grind-
ing rounds of toe-to-toe battling, Ali hurt Frazier badly
in the ninth round with a left hook. Frazier was fuckin'
dazed and confused.

Sensing the kill, Ali was fuckin' all over him, pound-
ing Frazier to the fuckin' head. But Frazier survived the
round and staggered back to his corner, where he got
the smelling salts.

In the tenth round, you could see Ali's offensive out-
put in the previous round had sapped both fighters. Frazier still seemed unfocused and Ali was lethargic with
fatigue.

It was Frazier who snapped out of the funk first, in
the twelfth round. He hurt Ali again and again with the
same right-jab/left-hook combo. Ali, as Frazier had earlier, barely survived the round.

Now both fighters were out on their feet. For two
and a half rounds they tried to gather up the strength
to throw the one punch it would take to finish the other,
clinching and leaning in a fuckin' hostile slow dance.

Then it fuckin' happened. Smokin' Joe captured some
fuckin' lightning in a bottle. It was the kind of punch
that, if it had been in a fucking *Rocky* movie, you never
would have fuckin' believed it.

Frazier knocked Ali down in the fifteenth round with
the single most devastating left hook in the fuckin' history of the fight game. By the time Ali's ass hit the fuckin'
canvas, he was three-quarters fuckin' way to la-la.

Ali's pretty face was already swollen from the blow. I personally think it busted his jaw. Hard to believe in this day and age, but Ali got up. That was because he had heart. They both had hearts the size of Brownsville and East New York put together. That left hook from hell was the last punch of the fight.

When Ali made it to his feet, Frazier did not attack him again but stood his ground and allowed the clock to run out. The fight ended with the men staring at each other, too fuckin' exhausted to move.

The gate at the Garden was a record $1,350,000, and that was just what they got at the box office. If you want to count the money that guys like me made off the fight, about a billion dollars were spent on fuckin' tickets. Don't seem likely that's ever gonna happen again.

I was lucky enough to see most of Ali's championship fights, either in person or on live closed circuit, which they used to have in those days. I followed his career from when he was Cassius Clay, before he fought Sonny Liston.

But today, like I said, Don King ruined the whole racket. There ain't no good fighters today. There's too many belts. Everybody's a fuckin' champion. They got a weight class for every fuckin' ounce!

Eight weight classes, eight champions. In the fuckin' world. That's all you need. Get rid of the fuckin' alphabet soup. The WBA, WBC, whatever the fuck. Toss 'em out. Let's make boxing pure. Then maybe we'd get some great fighters.

51. Delis Today

Here's another thing that ain't as good as it used to be: New York City delicatessens. How could they be? You got Indian people running your Jewish delis. You got Chinese workin' in Italian delis.

The original people don't want to do that kind of work no more. So they got to hire other people. The food, by far, isn't as good as it used to be. Today, everything is fuckin' precooked, or frozen. Then they reheat it. It's not like years ago when everything was made fresh at the deli. That's very hard to come by today.

I said, "Help me? Go fuckin' help yourself, you fuckin' A-rab cocksucker. You're stickin' that fuckin' finger up your ass and you fuckin' want to help me? Get the fuck out."

Just the other day, just before I started my fuckin' diet, I was in the fuckin' mood for a really good sandwich, so I decided to stop into a local delicatessen to see what fuckin' masterpiece I could have the guy behind the counter build.

Instead of the Italian guy who owns the place and cares about the quality of the product, there was this fuckin'

A-rab guy and he got his fuckin' fingers two knuckles deep up his fuckin' nose.

He was scratchin' his fuckin' ass. He had a fuckin' apron on that was so fuckin' dirty that you might have thought he worked in a fuckin' gas station. It was black with fuckin' dirt, like grime. It was fuckin' filthy.

"Can I help you, sir?" the fuckin' A-rab said. "Can I help you?"

I said, "Help me? Go fuckin' help yourself, you fuckin' A-rab cocksucker. You're stickin' that fuckin' finger up your ass and you fuckin' want to help me? Get the fuck out."

And I walked out of there.

But that's what you get today. I blame the fuckin' owners of these fuckin' delis. Instead of hiring a good deli guy, they hire the cocksucking A-rab with his fuckin' finger up his fuckin' ass.

It's because the guys who own the fucking delicatessens are cheap bastards. Instead of paying the thirty, forty dollars an hour it would take to get a decent deli guy in there, they hire the fuckin' A-rab for fuckin' minimum wage.

Because that's what you get for fuckin' five dollars an hour, a fuckin' A-rab grease monkey. They want this guy to make me a fuckin' corned beef sandwich. The fuckin' guy looked like he hadn't taken a fuckin' bath in a fuckin' week. Never mind a week. A fuckin' month.

And the fuckin' perspiration. You could smell him across the fuckin' room.

But in the fuckin' long run, I jumps up and bites them in the fuckin' ass, the cheap fucking deli store bastards.

Because nobody goes to their fuckin' deli anymore. Who wants a sandwich made by a filthy motherfucker?

Those deli guys can go fuck themselves. I walked out of the fuckin' joint, and the next time you get disgusted by the fuckin' conditions in a place, you should walk the fuck out, too.

52. Terrorist Assholes

You want to know my opinion? Here it is. I think the Muslim terrorist assholes want to hurt us a little bit. Because they don't like us, and they get fuckin' satisfaction out of it.

But they don't want to annihilate us. Because if they annihilated us, that's the end of the fuckin' world. If you really think about it, without the United States the world would come to a fuckin' end.

I mean, without the United States, who's gonna buy all the fuckin oil? The Chinese? What the fuck would

> *I mean, without the United States, who's gonna buy all the fuckin' oil? The Chinese? What the fuck would they pay for it with, a rice paddy?*

they pay for it with, a rice paddy? Without us they're fuckin' dead.

We feed half the fuckin' world, for Chrissake. Everybody would fuckin' starve. The whole fuckin' world economy would collapse. It would be like the fuckin' Roman times.

They want to hurt us a little bit so we'll give them fuckin' things for free, but they don't want to fuckin' destroy us. Destroy us and they know it's the end of the world as they know it.

What happens to all the pimps and whores? In some of these fuckin' countries, they'll fuck you for a fuckin' Tootsie Roll. I mean, without us, they'd be out of fuckin' business.

53. Christmas Sucks Lately

Now I love the holidays, you know. I ain't no fuckin' Scrooge, but the thing that pisses me off about the holidays is all the fuckin' time I got to spend with my relatives, and, even worse, Mona's fuckin' relatives.

There's always a few that you got to put up with even though you can't stand. They're cheap. They're miserly people. Unfortunately, around the holidays you got to be around these people.

These are the fuckin' people who, if its fifteen degrees outside and even colder with the fuckin' wind chill factor, they keep the fuckin' thermostat at fifty-five. You got to wear an overcoat in the fuckin' house.

And God forbid you should want something to drink when you're in their house. You can sit there for five hours and they won't even fuckin' offer you a glass of water—from the fuckin' tap.

And they always got the excuse: "We ran out of food. I didn't get a chance to go fucking shopping today." They been tellin' that same story for the last thirty fuckin' years, the cheap bastards.

People nowadays they even get offended if you wish 'em a Merry Christmas. I don't want to be around people like that. I don't want to live in a fuckin' world where you can't tell people Merry Christmas.

> *He almost got fired for wearing a fuckin' Santa cap, but if he'd been wearing a suicide belt or a fuckin' burka, nobody'd give a shit.*

There was a bus driver out on Long Island who wore a Santa cap to work one day during the holiday season. He gave it the old ho-ho-ho, and said Merry Christmas to the kids riding the bus in the morning.

And there was this one snot-nosed kid who got offended by what the fuckin' bus driver said. He complained to his fuckin' parents and they almost got the poor guy fired for wearing a fuckin' Santa cap.

Face it, that's what the world has come to today. He almost got fired for wearing a fuckin' Santa cap, but if he'd been wearing a suicide belt or a fuckin' burka, no-body'd give a shit.

The war on Christmas is everywhere. It's even got-ten as far as the post office. I guess it was the same everywhere, back when I was a kid and it came time to send Christmas cards, the post office sold special stamps. Some stamps had religious symbols on them. But not all of them were religious, just stamps that expressed the joy of Christmas. There were stamps with Santa Clauses on there, some with mistle-fuckin'-toe.

Well, I went to the post office this past December to get Christmas stamps and they gave me garbage, stamps with pictures of fucking snowflakes on them. I don't give a fuck what anybody says, a picture of a goddamn snow-flake is not a fuckin' Christmas stamp. C'mon. Give me a fucking break. I swear to God it looks more like a fuckin' ink spot. There's no fuckin' Christmas about it.

I want a real fuckin' Christmas stamp. I want a pic-ture of a fuckin' Santa Claus or a Rudolph the fuckin' Red-Nosed Reindeer. I mean, c'mon! It's the end of the fucking world.

What are they gonna do next, tell Rockefeller Cen-ter that they can't have a fuckin' Christmas tree every year? I'm tired of this fucking shit. Christmas is a fun holiday for everybody. And if you don't like it, go fuck yourself, go back to where the fuck you came from, you rat fuckin' bastards.

54. How Come the United States Can't Be More Like That Israel?

Last year I think it was, the Palestinian rat bastards kidnapped two Israeli soldiers. Two soldiers. That's all. And Israel started a fucking war. To get *two* soldiers back, they invaded a whole fucking country. They fired rockets. They dropped bombs. They sent the fucking infantry in there to clear out the Palestinian motherfuckers.

You know, the Big Man has got to tip his hat to these

Here I am delivering some swag (probably bootleg cigarettes) to Scrappy Bernstein's candy store. Scrappy's dog Meshugah (*left*) doesn't give a shit. (Photo courtesy Brian Merlis, www.brooklyn pix.com)

> *You bomb them with a fucking nuke, the fucking Chinese and the fucking Russians, they'll go running like a bunch of cock-a-roaches.*

fuckin' people. The United States wouldn't have the walnuts to try anything like that. Chances are we wouldn't do shit, just sit around with our thumbs up our fucking asses and stupid expressions on our faces.

The enemy could kidnap our soldiers, parade them around in front of cameras. Cut their balls off, rape them, do whatever the fuck they want to them, and what are we going to do? Nothing. If some A-rab cocksucker were to kidnap me and take me to Iraq, you could fuckin' kiss my fuckin' ass good-bye. I know this fucking country ain't gonna do nothing for me. They'd let me fuckin' die over there.

What's the reason we don't fuckin' retaliate? What are we afraid of? Starting World War III? Fuck it! You bomb them with a fucking nuke, the fucking Chinese and the fucking Russians, they'll go running like a bunch of cock-a-roaches.

That's how you fuckin' do business with these people. It's just like the old neighborhoods back in Brooklyn. If you were an outsider and you came in there and you robbed somebody, or started fuckin' trouble, they'd get fuckin' baseball bats and they'd beat the living shit out of you if they didn't fuckin' kill you.

That's what we got to do today. We got to kill these motherfuckers. Give 'em the fucking business. You gonna let them get away with this fucking bullshit? As long as you let 'em, they are gonna piss on you.

Take it from the Big Man, you got to fuck 'em where they breathe. Man, I'd press that fuckin' nuke button. Man, they'd be prayin' to fucking Allah. I'd blow them all the fuck up. I'd blow them out of the fucking sky.

I want you to write your congressman and the fucking president and ask, "How come when they kidnap American soldiers we don't go in there and fuckin' retaliate? It's fucking bullshit."

Protect our young men and women. I mean, they are our blood! Protect them!

55. Italians Pay Cash—So Fuck You

Me, I'm a cash type of guy. I like the green. The fuckin' moolah. I don't believe in no fuckin' plastic. If I go into a furniture store, a clothing store, a supermarket, I pay with cash, you know?

The other day I went into the La-Z-Boy to buy a couple of recliners, a couple of tables, and a rug my wife wanted. The guy said, that'll be forty-two hundred dollars. I took out forty-two hundred-dollar bills.

He said there's sixty dollars fuckin' tax, so I gave him three twenties. The guy calls his fuckin' manager. There's some kind of problem. This guy is looking like I just escaped from fuckin' Sing Sing.

Manager comes over and I can hear the fuckin' whispers. "This guy's paying in cash. He's an Italian guy. His name is Caracciolo. He must be with the fuckin' Mafia."

So I said, "Listen, forget about it. Give me back my money you fuckin' prick. What do you think, that every fuckin' Italian is with the fuckin' Mafia? Just because I pay in fuckin' cash, unlike the rest of these cocksuckers that pay with a fuckin' plastic credit card?"

"We're sorry," the manager said.

"Sorry?" I said. "Fuck you, you're sorry. Give me my fuckin' money back."

It just goes to show you how much fuckin' prejudice there is in the fuckin' world today. You go into a fuckin' store with cash and right away they think you're with the fuckin' Mafia.

They got some pair of balls, you know? I ought to take a broomstick and stick it up their fuckin' asses.

Another day I had to go to the bank. I had to cash a check.

And the fuckin' guy says, "Could I see some identification, please."

It was one of these banks over here in Fort Lee, New Jersey. And I pull out my fuckin' ID and show it to the guy. I can see him reading my name, trying to fuckin' pronounce it in his head. His brow's getting all fuckin' furrowed, and I can see the fuckin' wheels turning around inside his fuckin' head. Then I can see he's comin' to a fuckin' conclusion.

Mafia.

I said, "Listen here, you fuckin' bank-teller cocksucker, you got some fuckin' pair of balls. You know, I ought to have you thrown the fuck out of this fuckin' place. Fuck you, ass wipe."

I went over to the fuckin' manager, and I said, "Your fuckin' teller has got a fuckin' set of balls on him. Because I'm an Italian-American and I'm trying to cash a check he thinks I must be with the fuckin' Mafia. What kind of fucking bullshit is that? You can take this whole fuckin' bank and throw it in the fuckin' garbage. You're gonna have a fuckin' lawsuit on your hands."

Anyway, if you're Italian and you like to pay in cash like me, right away they're gonna think you are the fuckin' Mafia, too. They're full of shit. Forget about it.

56. Getting Robbed at Yankee Stadium

A friend of mine and his kid who went to Yankee Stadium on Bat Day and it took 'em two and a half fuckin' hours just to get through the fuckin' turnstiles.

Well, I went to Yankee Stadium the other day, and it didn't take me that long to get in. I had my problems after I got inside the fuckin' place. I went to the concession stand. I ordered a hotdog. I ordered a beer. The guy said eleven dollars. I put my hands up over my head and I just stood there, reaching for the fuckin' sky.

They said, "Sir, you are either going to have to pay or move along."

> *This fuckin' Steinbrenner cock-sucker, he's got all the fuckin' money in the fuckin' world. He's got all the fuckin' Yankee tickets and he's raising the prices way up.*

But I just stood there with my arms up over my head. I waited.

Finally a cop shows up and asks me what the fuck is wrong. "Whatsamatta?" fuckin' cop said.

"Whatsamatta? I'm just got fuckin' *robbed*," I said. "Five dollars for a raw hotdog? Six fuckin' dollars for some piss-warm beer?"

So let me ask you a question. This fuckin' Steinbrenner cocksucker, he's got all the fuckin' money in the fuckin' world. He's got all the fuckin' Yankee tickets and he's raising the prices way up.

He's got the fuckin' YES cable station. He's got every fuckin' thing—and now he's got to scalp the common working man for a fuckin' hotdog and a beer. Forty-five dollars for a fuckin' Yankee cap. Fifty fuckin' dollars for a Yankee T-shirt.

That's some set of fuckin' balls. He's telling the working man to stay the fuck away from his ballpark because he can't fuckin' afford to go to games anymore, the fuckin' working man who for generation after fuckin' generation has been the fuckin' backbone of baseball, the fuckin' national pastime.

How's a guy these days gonna take his wife and kids to Yankee Stadium and buy 'em hotdogs and soda? Fuckin' ice cream. Souvenirs. You got to plan on blowing three, four hundred dollars.

You got to give the working man a break, Georgie! You're not doing the right fucking thing. You're selling piss-warm fucking beer, warm fuckin' soda, raw fuckin' hotdogs, and you're robbin' people. Hey, George, what the fuck are you going to do with all that money?

Are you going to take it to the fucking grave with you? Think about it, folks. Every time you go to Yankee Stadium, and you go to them fuckin' concession stands, put your fuckin' hands up in the air and stand there. Take it from the fuckin' Big Man, you stand there until the fuckin' cop comes over, and you say, "I'm getting robbed here!"

Bring your own fuckin' sandwiches to the ballpark. That'll make the lines at the concession stand grow short in a fuckin' hurry. That's the way we did it in the old fuckin' days, back when I was a kid going to Ebbets Field in Brooklyn. Bring your own fuckin' salami. If they try and stop you, tell 'em to go fuck themselves.

57. Suzanne Somers

That bimbo from *Three's Company*, Suzanne Somers, her home burned down in one of them California wildfires. So, what does she say? "It could have been worse. I could have lost a son in Iraq."

And they say blondes aren't fuckin' dumb. Hey, Suzy, sorry your fuckin' house burned down—but your hooters, they still look pretty fuckin' good, so have a nice day.

58. Girls Going Wild

I know that all around the fuckin' country and even the fuckin' world the number one place that everybody wants to be on New Year's Eve is Times Square to watch the fuckin' ball drop.

Every year they base the TV shows from there and the mayor of the fuckin' city—whoever the fuck it is at the time, don't make no difference—says that there are one point five million people crammed into Times Square.

Then they put the TV cameras on the crowd and there's about forty thousand people sardined cruelly into these corrals with police barriers. It looks like these people are cattle waiting to get branded.

Give a girl $5 and she'll show you her tits.

I hope those people are at least high or something, because they don't let you drink and they don't let you in if you're already fuckin' drunk. So Times Square is a sober affair.

Now at least back in my day, there was a real party going on. Everybody was getting fuckin' hammered and doin' drugs and behaving in a bizarre manner. It was just like that whatchamacallit down there in New Orleans, Mardi Gras.

Back when I was in Times Square for the New Year, they'd have women who exposed their breasts. You always had to give them something. It was small-time shit but the meter was even running then. It was never much, though. I was usually amateur time pretending to be professional time. You'd give the fuckin' girl a fuckin' Marlboro and she'd show you her tits for about five fuckin' seconds.

Some of the women would flash their tits for free, later on as the frenzy of the impending ball-drop grew, but those were the fuckin' bimbos who'd been sucking too hard off their boyfriends' Jack Daniel's bottle.

Down in New Orleans it was worse, though. It was worse than just show-me-your-tits. I actually seen women fucking—actually having sex—right there on the street in New Orleans.

Guy'd give them a Marlboro, or maybe a five-dollar bill and they'd spread 'em right there in the street.

It was sick shit but as long as she was down there with her legs spread, there were plenty of guys willing to stand in fucking line, each with a fuckin' Marlboro and a five-dollar bill, ready to dip their fuckin' carrot.

The fuckin' bimbo was down there and I don't know

what the fuck she was doing with the five-dollar bills but she was smoking the goddamn cigarettes even as she was getting her eggs poached.

I tell you, people, it's amazing what a couple of shots of alcohol will do to the fucking mind. You give some women a couple of shots of alcohol and they're worse than men. Fuck, fuck, fuck. And then fuck some more. They're at least just as bad as men. I shouldn't make men seem innocent, because they ain't.

It's just that people think that women, and even girls, are innocent, and that ain't true, neither. Just watch one of them fuckin' *Girls Gone Wild* videos and you'll see what the fuck I mean.

59. What's Wrong with the People of Minnesota?

What the monkeyfuck is wrong with the fuckin' people of Minnesota? I know it gets cold there and it snows a lot but, jeez, those people are nuts, especially when it comes to going to the fucking voting booth.

People from Minnesota voted in a pro wrestler as their governor once, so I guess you can put anything past them. California keeps electing movie stars, so I guess they're just as fucked up.

Now the people of Minnesota have elected a Muslim. There was a big to-do because all elected officials in the fuckin' United States take the oath of office on a fuckin' Bible. Even the atheists. When a Jewish guy gets elected they still use a Bible, just a Jewish Bible, which is just the Old Testament.

Atheist politicians never fuckin' admit that they don't believe in God. They lie and tell their constituents that they are Christians, because that's how you get the most fuckin' votes.

Come to think of it, every fuckin' thing politicians do *ever* is to get the most votes. That's the fuckin' American way. But now they got an elected official in Minnesota who's saying no to the Bible. He needs a Koran. Well, this is a matter of some controversy until some flack announces that they found a Koran that once belonged to Thomas Jefferson.

Now I wasn't fuckin' born yesterday. I've been around the fuckin' block once or twice. How about you? How many of you believe that Thomas Jefferson had a Koran laying around the fuckin' house? Me, I never saw Thomas Jefferson as the "Praise Allah" type. I don't believe it, and I know you don't fuckin' believe it either. That's just the fuckin' story that they're puttin' around to shove in the public's mouth and keep us all fuckin' quiet.

60. Doctors Got Their Fuckin' Nerve

Doctors are my favorite. Who's got bigger balls than a doctor? Nobody. They push you the fuck around and they want you to be happy about it, too. Sure, they'll always give you an appointment. Doesn't matter if they've already got three appointments for three o'clock, they'll

Who's got bigger balls than a doctor? Nobody.

give you the three o'clock slot. Then they make you wait for an hour in the fuckin' waiting room before they call you.

You think you're gonna get to see the doctor at that point, but fuck no. They take you to another, smaller waiting room and they make you wait for another fuckin' hour, only now without a fuckin' magazine. Then at five fuckin' o'clock, two fuckin' hours after you get there, the fuckin' doctor finally sees you and he always says the same fuckin' thing, "Sorry, I had an emergency."

An emergency? A fuckin' emergency? This fuckin' doctor has a fuckin' emergency every fuckin' time I go to see him. Next time it fuckin' happens, I'll give him a fuckin' emergency right in his Hippocratic Oath.

Conclusion

A whole lot of years ago I went to my first bar mitzvah, Bernie Hockheiser's. If you don't know what a bar mitzvah is, it's like a holy communion for Jewish boys. At the age of thirteen, according to Jewish law, they are now men. Which doesn't mean they can vote or get a driver's license or get a drink in a bar or anything grown-up like that. Why the Jews picked the age of thirteen, when a guy is barely out of puberty, I don't know. Ask a rabbi.

It was quite a party. Bar mitzvahs are a big deal for the Jews, so Bernie's old man spared no expense. He bankrolled a huge bash at Mendelbaum's Catering Hall on Coney Island Avenue. I'd never seen so much food—there was enough chopped liver, Swedish meatballs, miniature wieners, and potato pancakes to feed a small country. There was an ice sculpture that squirted champagne and a big mold of Bernie made out of chopped liver. And that was just the warm-up for the main event—slabs of prime rib the size of a manhole cover, the whole nine yards. The booze flowed like Niagara Falls and everyone was doing all those great Jewish dances and raising

Bernie and his old man up on chairs, the whole ball of wax. It was, for a kid like me, the best I'd ever had.

I remember seeing this really old guy sitting at one of the tables. I mean, this guy was fuckin' ancient, ninety if he was a day. He was so old, nobody knew which side of the family he was from.

So this old guy, he motions for me to come over to the table. I trot on over there and he points to a chair and I sit. He leans over—I can still remember the smell of stuffed derma on his breath, and he says to me, "Young man, I am going to tell you the three things that everyone needs to know to live a happy life."

So I get kind of excited, you know—I mean, this old guy had obviously been around a few years and had a lot of life experience. I was thrilled that he wanted to share it with me. So I leaned in and he whispered those three things in my ear.

Well, a lot of years have gone by and I think I can say I've led a pretty good life, all things considered. And if I have one regret, it's this: I can't remember for shit what those three things were.

There's really no point to this story other than the fact that I didn't know how else to end this book. So consider it over. If you enjoyed it, I'm glad you got your money's worth. If you didn't enjoy this book, go fuck yourself.

And that's that.

You are now leaving Brooklyn. Go the fuck home. (Photo courtesy of Kevin Helmick)